The Gift of Repentance

God's Call for a Change of Heart

Kevin Perrotta

Published by The Word Among Us Press
7115 Guilford Road
Frederick, Maryland 21704
www.wau.org

ISBN: 978-1-59325-269-4
eISBN: 978-1-59325-464-3

Nihil Obstat: The Rev. Michael Morgan, Vicar General/Chancellor
Censor Librorum
November 14, 2014

Imprimatur: Most Rev. Felipe J. Estévez, Bishop of St. Augustine
November 14, 2014

Scripture texts used in this work are taken from the New Revised Standard Version
Bible: Catholic Edition, copyright © 1965 and 1966 by the Division of Christian
Education of the National Council of the Churches of Christ in the USA.
All rights reserved. Used with permission.

Excerpts from the English translation of the *Catechism of the Catholic Church*
for use in the United States of America, copyright © 1994, United States Catholic
Conference, Inc.—Libreria Editrice Vaticana. Used with permission.

Cover design: Andrea Alvarez
Cover art: Raphael, *The Miraculous Draught of Fishes*, 1515.
Credit: HIP/Art Resource, NY

Made and printed in the United States of America

Library of Congress Control Number: 2014951175

To Mike O'Brien and all the "peeps" at
Wolverine Crossfit, Ann Arbor, Michigan

Contents

Welcome to
The Word Among Us
Keys to the Bible

Have you ever lost your keys? Everyone seems to have at least one "lost keys" story to tell. Maybe you had to break a window of your house or wait for the auto club to let you into your car. Whatever you had to do probably cost you—in time, energy, money, or all three. Keys are definitely important items to have on hand!

The guides in The Word Among Us Keys to the Bible series are meant to provide you with a handy set of keys that can "unlock" the treasures of the Scriptures for you. Scripture is God's living word. Within its pages we meet the Lord. So as we study and meditate on Scripture and unlock its many treasures, we discover the riches it contains—and in the process, we grow in intimacy with God.

Since 1982, *The Word Among Us* magazine has helped Catholics develop a deeper relationship with the Lord through daily meditations that bring the Scriptures to life. More than ever, Catholics today desire to read and pray with the Scriptures, and many have begun to form small faith-sharing groups to explore the Bible together.

We designed the Keys to the Bible series after conducting a survey among our magazine readers to learn what they would want in a Catholic Bible study. We found that they were looking for easy-to-understand, faith-filled materials that approach Scripture from a clearly Catholic perspective. Moreover, they wanted a Bible study that would show them how they could apply what they learned from Scripture to their everyday lives. They also asked for sessions that they could complete in an hour or two.

Our goal was to design a simple, easy-to-use Bible study guide that is also challenging and thought-provoking. We hope that this guide fulfills those admittedly ambitious goals. We are confident, however, that taking the time to go through this guide—whether by yourself, with a friend, or in a small group—will be a worthwhile endeavor that will bear fruit in your life.

How to Use the Guides in This Series

The study guides in the Keys to the Bible series are divided into six sessions that each deal with a particular aspect of the topic. Before starting the first session, take the time to read the introduction, which sets the stage for the sessions that follow.

Whether you use this guide for personal reflection and study, as part of a faith-sharing group, or as an aid in your prayer time, be sure to begin each session with prayer. Ask God to open his word to you and to speak to you personally. Read each Scripture passage slowly and carefully. Then, take as much time as you need to meditate on the passage and pursue any thoughts it brings to mind. When you are ready, move on to the accompanying commentary, which offers various insights into the text.

Two sets of questions are included in each session to help you "mine" the Scripture passage and discover its relevance to your life. Those under the heading "Understand!" focus on the text itself and help you grasp what it means. Occasionally a question allows for a variety of answers and is meant to help you explore the passage from several angles. "Grow!" questions are intended to elicit a personal response by helping you examine your life in light of the values and truths that you uncover through your study of the Scripture passage and its setting. Under the headings "Reflect!" and "Act!" we offer suggestions to help you respond concretely to the challenges posed by the passage.

Finally, pertinent quotations from the Fathers of the Church, as well as insights from contemporary writers, appear throughout each session. Coupled with relevant selections from the *Catechism of the Catholic Church* and information about the history, geography, and culture of first-century Palestine, these selections (called "In the Spotlight") add new layers of understanding and insight to your study.

As is true with any learning resource, you will benefit the most from this study by writing your answers to the questions in the spaces provided. The simple act of writing can help you formulate your thoughts more clearly—and will also give you a record of your reflections and spiritual growth that you can return to in the future to see how much God has accomplished in your life. End your reading or study with a prayer thanking God for what you have learned—and ask the Holy Spirit to guide you in living out the call you have been given as a Christian in the world today.

Although the Scripture passages to be studied and the related verses for your reflection are printed in full in each guide (from the New Revised Standard Version: Catholic Edition), you will find it helpful to have a Bible on hand for looking up other passages and cross-references or for comparing different translations.

The format of the guides in The Word Among Us Keys to the Bible series is especially well suited for use in small groups. Some recommendations and practical tips for using this guide in a Bible discussion group are offered on pages 117–120.

We hope that this guide will unlock the meaning of true repentance—which is a change of heart—and lead you to experience the joy that it will bring in your life.

The Word Among Us Press

Introduction

An Uncomfortable Position

"God has given . . . the repentance that leads to life."
—Acts 11:18

There isn't a lot of grunting and groaning at the gym where I work out. The guys and gals generally sweat through even the toughest workouts in determined silence. But there is one exercise that elicits "ughs" and "arghs"—a routine called "Bring Sally Up." It involves loading an Olympic bar with as much weight as you can manage, getting it on your shoulders, and then standing or squatting with it—"Bring Sally up" or "Bring Sally down"—in accompaniment to music in which those two lines keep alternating. The tricky part is that the lines repeat irregularly, making the intervals between Sally's upping and downing unequal. At some points, you have to stay in the squat for quite a while. That's where the groaning occurs.

At one time or another, all of us find ourselves in a different uncomfortable position: weighed down by our sins. We become aware of how far we have fallen short of what God and other people reasonably expect of us—and of what we expect of ourselves. We have let people down or have hurt them, and we feel regret, disappointment with ourselves, sorrow, and maybe even a tinge of despair.

Distressing as it is, there is something to be gained by staying a while with the realization of our sins. Like squatting down with the Olympic bar, it can do a person good. It is a humble position, from which certain truths about ourselves and about God are easier to see.

In fact, feeling upset about our sins is a sign of moral health. Since we *are* sinners, feeling fine about everything we do would be moral insensitivity. When there is injury, a healthy body feels pain. When we have done wrong, the healthy conscience is troubled. This experience is valuable because it is the only starting point for the process that, with God's help, can lead us to change.

Paying Attention to Our Conscience

Conscience is where we look ahead to assess our options as good or bad and look back to evaluate our behavior. It is the place inside us where we are alone with God. This is why we do well to pay attention when our conscience is disturbed. The disturbance may be God trying to communicate with us. Obviously, consciousness of our sins is uncomfortable, but it is cause for hope. In those feelings of guilt, God is calling us to return to him!

If we stay with our disturbance over our sins, we will find that God has more to say to us than "You messed up." He wants to help us see ourselves more realistically, to recognize—and repudiate—the motives that lead us into sin, to grasp his saving love, to see the way toward living according to his goodness and grace. It's not an easy process. But if boosting fitness is worth a few groans, how much more is the process of repentance.

This does not mean that we should get depressed about ourselves—quite the opposite. Depression is useless since almost by definition, it means giving up. The sorrow over our sins that initiates the process of repentance leads not to losing heart but to a *change* of heart. Paul had this distinction in mind when he wrote, "Godly grief produces a repentance that leads to salvation and brings no regret, but worldly grief produces death" (2 Corinthians 7:10). Repentance may not clear away depression—which has many causes, some of them biological—but it is a step toward dealing with depression to the degree that our depression is fed by guilt and anger at ourselves.

Coming to a realization of ourselves as sinners puts us within range of hearing the gospel. The gospel—the good news—that Jesus announced is that God's reign over us is ready to break into our lives, to penetrate the deepest parts of our being. The good news that his apostles preached after Jesus' death and resurrection is that God's reign is now breaking into our lives through Jesus. We can experience it by faith in him and by Baptism.

The Effective Treatment for Sin

You know the kind of pamphlet sometimes found in doctor's waiting rooms—the kind with titles such as *Now That You Have Diabetes*? Pamphlets like that tend to follow a formula. In the past, they say, not much could be done for people with your condition. But today, with medical advances, the condition you have is often treatable; many people who have it go on to live long and active lives. The gospel is like those pamphlets, only much more so. Now that you've discovered you are a sinner, what can you expect? Left to itself, the condition is fatal. But now there is an entirely effective treatment: Jesus' death and resurrection and the gift of the Holy Spirit. So today it can be said with assurance that people who have your condition— and mine—can, by God's grace, live productive lives. But not only that: we can go on to live forever!

So it is with hope that we pay attention to the awareness within ourselves that we have sinned.

One way we hear God speaking to us in our conscience is through listening to his word in Scripture. "The Word of God alone can profoundly change man's heart," Pope Benedict XVI said. Thus, it is important that we "enter into ever increasing intimacy with his Word." To draw nourishment from the word of God, Benedict said, is our "first and fundamental task."

That's where this Bible study can help. While we have, so to speak, "brought Sally down," we can ponder six passages from the Bible. The first two are accounts of people going through a process of repentance. The third, a prayer, brings us inside the experience. These are from the Old Testament. Then from the New Testament are three passages focused on Jesus: on his call to a change of heart and life, on his death and resurrection as the way for us to experience this change, and on his friendship with us.

The first three readings spur us to reflect on our own experience of recognizing our sins, taking action against them, and beginning the journey of return to God. The second three direct our attention to Jesus as teacher, healer, and Savior. Jesus calls us to grow in love beyond anything that is easy or comfortable for us—and enables us to do it by nourishing us with himself.

I hope that my comments on the passages in each session will launch your exploration of the biblical texts and that the questions will help you consider how, through these texts, God is speaking to you. To aid your study, I have recorded short podcasts covering each session. You can find these at wau.org/repentance.

This raises a final question about this study: is it designed for reading and reflection during Lent? The answer is yes if it happens to be Lent, but no if you happen to be reading it at another time. That is to say that the biblical passages will work very well for reflection during Lent—or just before Lent when you are thinking about what to do during that season. But they will work equally well as a basis for reflection at any season or in any situation.

Kevin Perrotta

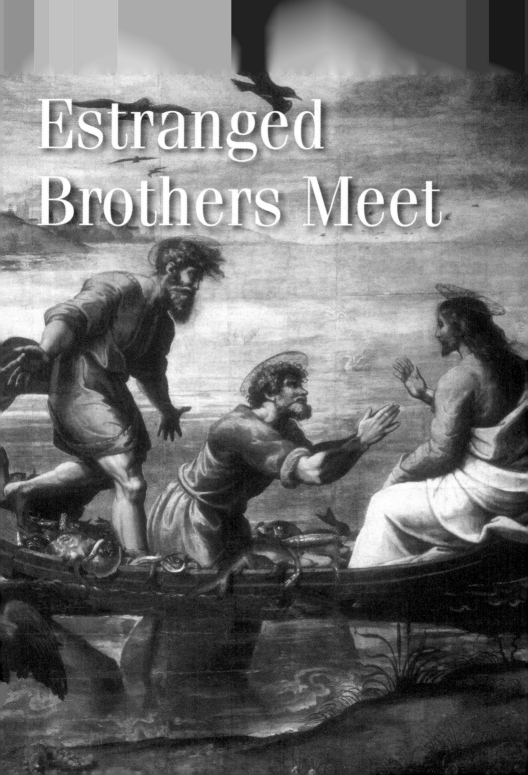

Estranged Brothers Meet

Genesis 44:18–45:15

⁴⁴:¹⁸Then Judah stepped up to him and said, "O my lord, let your servant please speak a word in my lord's ears. . . . ¹⁹My lord asked his servants, saying, 'Have you a father or a brother?' ²⁰And we said to my lord, 'We have a father, an old man, and a young brother, the child of his old age. His brother is dead; he alone is left of his mother's children, and his father loves him.' ²¹Then you said to your servants, 'Bring him down to me, so that I may set my eyes on him.' ²²We said to my lord, 'The boy cannot leave his father, for if he should leave his father, his father would die.' ²³Then you said to your servants, 'Unless your youngest brother comes down with you, you shall see my face no more.' ²⁴When we went back to your servant my father we told him the words of my lord. ²⁵And when our father said, 'Go again, buy us a little food,' ²⁶we said, ' . . . Only if our youngest brother goes with us, will we go down; for we cannot see the man's face unless our youngest brother is with us.' ²⁷Then your servant my father said to us, 'You know that my wife bore me two sons; ²⁸one left me, and I said, Surely he has been torn to pieces; and I have never seen him since. ²⁹If you take this one also from me, and harm comes to him, you will bring down my gray hairs in sorrow to Sheol.' ³⁰Now therefore, when I come to your servant my father and the boy is not with us, then, as his life is bound up in the boy's life, ³¹when he sees that the boy is not with us, he will die; and your servants will bring down the gray hairs of your servant our father with sorrow to Sheol. ³²For your servant became surety for the boy to my father, saying, 'If I do not bring him back to you, then I will bear the blame in the

> It is a far, far better thing that I do, than I have ever done before."
> — Sydney Carton, accepting execution in place of an innocent man. Charles Dickens, *A Tale of Two Cities*

sight of my father all my life.' [33]Now therefore, please let your servant remain as a slave to my lord in place of the boy; and let the boy go back with his brothers. [34]For how can I go back to my father if the boy is not with me? I fear to see the suffering that would come upon my father."

[45:1]Then Joseph could no longer control himself before all those who stood by him, and . . . [2]he wept. . . . [3]Joseph said to his brothers, "I am Joseph. Is my father still alive?" But his brothers could not answer him, so dismayed were they at his presence.

[4]Then Joseph said to his brothers, "Come closer to me." And they came closer. He said, "I am your brother, Joseph, whom you sold into Egypt. [5]And now do not be distressed, or angry with yourselves, because you sold me here; for God sent me before you . . . [7]to keep alive for you many survivors. [8]So it was not you who sent me here, but God; he has made me a father to Pharaoh, and lord of all his house and ruler over all the land of Egypt. [9]Hurry and go up to my father and say to him, 'Thus says your son Joseph, . . . come down to me, do not delay. . . . [11]I will provide for you. . . .'" . . . [14]Then he fell upon his brother Benjamin's neck and wept, while Benjamin wept upon his neck. [15]And he kissed all his brothers and wept upon them; and after that his brothers talked with him.

The first of our readings is the climax of a long chain of events. The story begins in Canaan—present-day Israel and Palestine— with a man named Jacob, who will become the ancestor of the people of Israel. Jacob has two wives and two concubines. One wife, Rachel, is his favorite. Jacob has two sons by her, and ten sons by the other three women. As the sons grow up, he treats Rachel's two boys as his favorites.

The elder of the favorite sons is named Joseph. Out of envy, the ten plot to get rid of him. At the suggestion of one of the brothers, Judah, they sell Joseph into slavery and then lead Jacob to think that Joseph was killed by a marauding animal. Jacob is inconsolable (Genesis 37:34-35).

Years pass. Joseph goes through various ups and downs in Egypt. Then, by an almost miraculous sequence of events, he ends up as the highest government official in Egypt. In the meantime, Judah loses two of his own sons.

After many years, a drought in Canaan drives the ten brothers to go to Egypt to buy food. When they arrive, they meet the government official in charge of food distribution: it is Joseph, although they do not recognize him. He recognizes them but does not reveal himself. He treats the brothers with a mixture of harshness and kindness, which leaves them frightened and confused. And he tells them that if they return to get more food in the future—as he knows they will—they won't get any unless Jacob's remaining favorite son, Benjamin, is with them.

> Does Joseph yearn for reconciliation with his brothers? Is he angry with them?

It is difficult to discern Joseph's motives for his peculiar treatment of his brothers. Does he yearn for reconciliation with them? Is he angry with them? Does he want revenge? Perhaps, in fact, he is ambivalent: he feels impelled to welcome and care for them, yet he is bitter toward them. So he supplies them with food for their families, yet he keeps himself concealed from them and plays scary games with them. Eventually, the brothers do make a second visit to Egypt, this time with Benjamin. By a trick, Joseph then frames Benjamin as a thief, which brings us up to our reading.

Joseph has just declared his intention of punishing Benjamin by keeping him as his slave in Egypt. But the other brothers are free to go home, as he says, in "peace to [their] father" (Genesis 44:17). Of course, both Joseph and the brothers well know there will be no peace at home if they arrive without Benjamin.

At this point, Judah steps forward to speak. We might expect him to say something like "Our families are anxious and hungry. We've got to get home with the food. Too bad about Benjamin. Go easy on him."

But that isn't what Judah says.

"My lord," Judah begins—a respectful way of addressing someone higher on the social ladder, just as "your servant" is a submissive way of referring to oneself. He reminds Joseph that the brothers have brought Benjamin to Egypt only because he had insisted on it when they made their first trip. Judah explains Jacob's attachment to Benjamin. Not only is the boy a child of Jacob's only beloved wife, but he also is the only *remaining* child of this wife, her other son having disappeared years ago.

Joseph—that son who disappeared—listens attentively. He had never known what happened back home when his father learned of his disappearance. Now he discovers the truth. As Old Testament scholar W. Lee Humphreys says, "The anguished cry of his father (Genesis 37:33) rings out again as it is heard once more in Judah's recollection."

Jacob's favoritism toward Joseph and Benjamin has been a bitter, lifelong fact for Judah. But whatever envy Judah has felt toward these favored brothers—and whatever anger at his father—he now leaves behind. Jacob will not change; he will love some of his children less than others. It is painful for the son who is not the favored one, but this is Jacob's way, and Judah, the slighted son, accepts his father as the flawed man that he is.

As Judah tells Joseph that his father's life is bound up with his favored son Benjamin, we can see that Judah's heart has become bound up with his father's. Judah feels his father's anxiety over Benjamin as well as his love for him. Indeed, Judah feels his father's *preference* for Benjamin.

In effect, he assents to it and presents it to the Egyptian official as the reason why he should let Benjamin go home.

Judah appeals to Joseph for mercy, not so much for Benjamin as for his father and for himself. "How can I go back to my father if the boy is not with me? I fear to see the suffering that would come upon my father" (Genesis 44:34). Judah can envision what will happen when the brothers arrive home: it will be a terrible replay of the announcement of Joseph's disappearance. Judah can imagine his father's grief-stricken face, and he recoils; he would do anything to avoid causing his father such pain again. Thus, Judah would experience becoming Joseph's slave as an act of mercy to *himself,* because it would enable him to save his father from grief. What a change of heart Judah has come to!

Unknown to Judah, his offer strikes Joseph to the heart. Here before him, Joseph sees the less favored son pleading for the father who has slighted him. What does this say to Joseph, the favored son? Joseph has worked at forgetting his father. But now he is forced to ask himself how he, the favored son, can love their father less than the less favored Judah?

Looking at Judah's face contorted by anguish at the thought of their father's suffering, Joseph can imagine how Jacob will react if the brothers come home without Benjamin. The vision releases Joseph's tightly coiled self-control. He can no longer conceal his identity from his brothers. "I am Joseph," he declares (Genesis 45:3).

The brothers are terrified. This powerful Egyptian official is the brother they had sold into slavery! But the brothers are not Joseph's immediate concern. Finally moved at the thought of his father's grief, Joseph now reaches out to him. With a force that makes the brothers tremble, he cries out, "Is my father still alive?" (Genesis 45:3).

Still, Joseph must think about his brothers. What will he do with them? Pay them back for the suffering they have inflicted on him? Be reconciled with them? Right up to this moment, Joseph may not have resolved the question in his own mind.

If it is to be reconciliation, there must be some dealing with the wrong they have done him. It cannot be swept under a rug. But what is Joseph to do with the bitter memory of all he has suffered from their crime against him?

Without realizing it, Judah has pointed the way by his readiness to accept suffering for the welfare of their father. Is *Joseph* willing to accept suffering for the sake of his father, and brothers? It is not a question of taking on new suffering but of embracing the suffering already endured. Rather than seeing his enslavement as cause for retribution, will he view it as part of the process that has now put him in the position to save his family from starvation? It is not that he would regard being sold into slavery as a good thing, but is he willing to perceive God's hand in that evil event? Will he accept his suffering retroactively, as part of God's plan, and in this way set aside anger toward his brothers?

Yes, he will. Joseph announces his change of heart. "God sent me before you to preserve for you a remnant on earth, and to keep alive for you many survivors. So it was not you who sent me here, but God" (Genesis 45:7-8).

As Joseph speaks, we may picture Judah looking intently at the suddenly recognizable face of his younger brother and glimpsing his suffering as a slave in Egypt. Indeed, having put away envy on one side and anger on the other, the two brothers can look each other in the eyes, perhaps for the first time.

Understand!

1. Jacob's favored wife, Rachel, bore Joseph and Benjamin. The other ten brothers were sons of the second wife and two concubines. When Jacob says to these ten brothers, "You know that my wife bore me two sons" (Genesis 44:27), what would that indicate to them about his feelings for their mothers? About his feelings toward them, his other sons?

   _____

   _____

   _____

   _____

   _____

   _____

2. At the end of his appeal to the Egyptian official he does not recognize as Joseph, Judah abandons the polite "your servant my father" and "your servant" for the more direct "My father" and "I" (Genesis 44:30, 32, 34). What does this suggest about Judah's state of mind?

   _____

   _____

   _____

   _____

   _____

   _____

3. Keeping in mind that Judah does not know that the Egyptian official he is speaking to is his brother Joseph, why does he think that this powerful official might be persuaded by what he tells him about his family situation?

_____

_____

_____

_____

_____

4. From the difference between Joseph's expression of emotion toward his brothers and their response to him (Genesis 45:14-15), what would you conclude about the brothers' attitude toward him?

_____

_____

_____

_____

_____

5. Joseph discerns God's presence in events that have led up to this confrontation of brothers (Genesis 45:5, 7-8). Where else in this reading can you discern God's presence?

_____

_____

_____

_____

_____

▶ In the Spotlight
Where Is Sheol?

When Jacob talks with his sons about their going to Egypt a second time, they remind him of the requirement set by the Egyptian official (Joseph, unrecognized by them) on their first purchasing trip to Egypt. The official will not admit them to his presence again unless they bring their youngest brother, Benjamin. Jacob strongly objects to their taking Benjamin with them to Egypt. After the disappearance of Joseph, Benjamin is the only remaining child of his favorite wife, Rachel. "If you take this one also from me, and harm comes to him," Jacob tells his sons, "you will bring down my gray hairs in sorrow to Sheol" (Genesis 44:29).

What, and where, is Sheol?

The Hebrew word "Sheol" (it rhymes with "the hole") refers to the realm of the dead. After death, the Israelites thought, while the body rots away, the personality goes down under the earth to a place of darkness—Sheol. Residents of Sheol are lifeless shadows of their former selves. They experience neither reward nor punishment. All are in a condition of inactivity—not in the positive sense of rest, but in the negative sense of having lost any capacity to act (see, for example, Psalms 6:5; 31:17; 49:15; and also Job 3:16-19).

For most of the Old Testament period, Sheol is how the Israelites conceived of the condition of the dead. Toward the end of this period, however, through divine revelation Jews began to realize that God has resurrection in store for those who obey and serve him. Those who refuse to obey God destine themselves to a painful condition of separation from him. But Jacob lived long before the revelation of final judgment after death and resurrection. For him, to go down to Sheol in sorrow would simply have meant ending his whole life in unalterable grief. It is that which Judah is willing to do anything to prevent. Even if his worldview is too small, his love is admirable!

Grow!

1. Between the day when Judah leads the brothers in selling Joseph into slavery and the day he begs Joseph to let him take Benjamin's place as a slave, Judah has experienced the loss of two of his adult sons (Genesis 38:7, 10). How might this experience affect the way he relates to his father in this session's reading? When has suffering opened your eyes to others' pain?

   _____

   _____

   _____

   _____

   _____

2. When Judah and the brothers had gotten rid of Joseph, they apparently thought that Jacob would get over his grief at the loss of this favorite son. But this was a miscalculation (Genesis 37:34-35). Now Judah has a realistic view of the impact that losing Benjamin would have on his father (44:30-31). What helps children come to understand their parents? Have you come to a more rounded view of your parents as you have gotten older? How has this affected how you relate to them?

   _____

   _____

   _____

   _____

   _____

3. As children, we have needs and expectations that our parents sometimes fail to meet. Consider Judah and the other brothers who were slighted by their father. Yet Judah is willing to let go of

resentment toward his father for his failings. What decisions may be involved in loving our parents despite their not having loved us as we would have wanted? Where are you in this process?

_____

_____

_____

_____

_____

_____

4. Judah's offer to take Benjamin's place in slavery is probably the finest moment in his life. Would he have come to this mature love for his brother—and his father—if he had not earlier taken part in selling Joseph into slavery? In what ways can our sins, when we have repented of them, play a part in making us better people? What has been your experience of this?

_____

_____

_____

_____

_____

_____

5. Judah is willing to suffer in Benjamin's place. When have you accepted suffering to relieve someone else's pain? When have you wished you could do so, but couldn't? How have these experiences affected you?

_____

_____

_____

_____

_____

_____

▶ In the Spotlight
Can Pain Open Our Eyes?

Between the time when Judah advised his brothers to sell Joseph into slavery and the moment when he offered to take Benjamin's place in slavery, Judah suffered the sudden loss of two of his adult sons. The biblical author does not make an explicit connection, but it seems possible that Judah's bereavement opened his heart to compassion for his father, Jacob. Before the death of his own sons, Judah did not take much concern for how the loss of Joseph would affect Jacob. Afterward, however, when Jacob was in danger of losing Benjamin, Judah tried desperately to protect his father from experiencing such grief again.

The nineteenth-century Russian writer Leo Tolstoy explored the mysterious way that suffering can break through hardness of heart in a story entitled *The Death of Ivan Ilych*. Ivan's main goal is to enjoy life in a manner that draws the admiration of other people. He is a judge but has only a slight concern for justice. The law is merely the sphere in which he makes a substantial income and gains people's approval for his skill in handling difficult cases. Ivan marries not because he is in love but because it is the expected thing to do, and he assumes it will be pleasant. His greatest delight is a card game, bridge. He has no deep concern for anyone except himself.

Then Ivan bruises his back in a fall from a ladder. At first it seems unimportant, but soon he loses his appetite and begins to feel a gnawing pain. His deterioration shreds the fabric of his comfortable life. As he becomes seriously ill, he realizes that his wife and grown-up daughter find him to be a burden. Hardly anyone except his young son and a teenage servant boy has any feeling for him at all.

As Ivan's pain ratchets up and his loneliness intensifies, a question occurs to him: has he lived in the right way? Of course, he tells himself. After all, he has always conducted himself according to the values of the people around him. But his unrelenting pain drills the question into him. Finally, as he gasps for breath on his last day, he comes to this awful recognition: yes indeed, his life has been misspent. And then, only in his final hour, does he realize what *is* the right way to live. It is the way of compassion! And so, as he dies, Ivan tries, wordlessly, to show his pity for his grief-stricken son and even his uncaring wife.

The entire story is available at the Christian Classics Ethereal Library website (ccel.org).

Reflect!

1. Where are the broken relationships in your life? What are you willing to do to seek restoration? What steps could you take? Judah's desire to care for his father led him to an action that opened the way to reconciliation between Joseph and his brothers. What inspiration do you find here for dealing with a damaged relationship in your own life?

2. Regarding Judah's willingness to substitute himself for Benjamin as Joseph's slave, biblical scholar Claus Westermann says, "The Bible speaks for the first time of vicarious suffering." As you consider this idea of suffering on behalf of others, reflect on this prophecy pointing toward Jesus:

> For he grew up before him like a young plant,
>   and like a root out of dry ground;
> he had no form or majesty that we should look at him,
>   nothing in his appearance that we should desire him.
> He was despised and rejected by others;
>   a man of suffering and acquainted with infirmity;
> and as one from whom others hide their faces

he was despised, and we held him of no account.
Surely he has borne our infirmities
    and carried our diseases;
yet we accounted him stricken,
    struck down by God, and afflicted.
But he was wounded for our transgressions,
    crushed for our iniquities;
upon him was the punishment that made us whole,
    and by his bruises we are healed.
All we like sheep have gone astray;
    we have all turned to our own way,
and the Lord has laid on him
    the iniquity of us all.

He was oppressed, and he was afflicted,
    yet he did not open his mouth;
like a lamb that is led to the slaughter,
    and like a sheep that before its shearers is silent,
    so he did not open his mouth.
By a perversion of justice he was taken away.
    Who could have imagined his future?
For he was cut off from the land of the living,
    stricken for the transgression of my people.
They made his grave with the wicked
    and his tomb with the rich,
although he had done no violence,
    and there was no deceit in his mouth.

Yet it was the will of the Lord to crush him with pain.
When you make his life an offering for sin,
    he shall see his offspring, and shall prolong his days;
through him the will of the Lord shall prosper.
    Out of his anguish he shall see light;
he shall find satisfaction through his knowledge.

> The righteous one, my servant, shall make many
>   righteous,
>   and he shall bear their iniquities.
> Therefore I will allot him a portion with the great,
>   and he shall divide the spoil with the strong;
> because he poured out himself to death,
>   and was numbered with the transgressors;
> yet he bore the sin of many,
>   and made intercession for the transgressors.
>   (Isaiah 53:2-12)

Now reflect on these words of Jesus about himself:

> Jesus called [his disciples] and said to them, "You know
> that among the Gentiles those whom they recognize as their
> rulers lord it over them, and their great ones are tyrants over
> them. But it is not so among you; but whoever wishes to
> become great among you must be your servant, and whoever
> wishes to be first among you must be slave of all. For the
> Son of Man came not to be served but to serve, and to give
> his life as a ransom for many." (Mark 10:42-45)

▶ In the Spotlight
The Struggle to Forgive

Would Joseph forgive the brothers who had inflicted years of
suffering on him? Laura (not her real name) faced this question.
Several years and several children into her marriage, her husband
became distant. Not only was he away from home long hours at
his job, but his emotional detachment from her and the children
became so pronounced that she wondered whether he had a
personality disorder. Here is her story:

During those years, I could tell that God was pulling me through. Even at my lowest points, I never felt separated from God's love. Always, there in my laundry room, was an image of Jesus as the Divine Mercy. I meditated on it again and again in those long lonely times, and though it grew worn and tattered, it never failed to comfort and calm me.

Then, after fifteen years of coldness and indifference, my husband began to express more interest in our family life. As if he were coming out of a dream world, he paid much more attention to me and our children. In fact, he became a real family man, and our marriage and home life changed remarkably. I began to feel his love.

Those mysterious years of coldness receded into the background. We celebrated our twenty-fifth anniversary, our fortieth, and our fiftieth as a happily married couple.

Then our son was in a serious accident and had to be taken to the hospital. And as we kept vigil over him, my husband launched into a confession. He poured out the sorry tale that explained those fifteen bewildering years of our marriage. During the whole period, he had been carrying on an affair with his secretary. I could hardly believe my ears.

He said that after fifteen guilt-free years of lying and deceiving, something touched his conscience. Finally aware of the horrible state of his soul, he sought out a priest and made the most sincere confession of his life. Tremendous peace washed over him, and he felt unchained and strengthened to begin a new life. He broke with his secret lover, returned to his family, and never looked back.

If my husband had taken out a knife and stabbed me, I could hardly have been more hurt. Incredible as it may sound, never once had I suspected adultery. I had trusted him absolutely.

Our son went on to complete recovery, but it has taken me much longer to heal from the deep wounds I received that day. For months afterwards, I screamed in fury. "I loved you and you double-crossed me! How could you do that to me?" Fine for him to have made his peace with God. But what about all those years I spent in anguish?

I was angry with myself for having been so naïve. I was even angry with God. Why hadn't he intervened sooner?

My husband begged forgiveness a thousand times, but I just couldn't find it in me, even though I admitted my anger every time I went to confession. "You have to forgive him," the priest would say. "I don't have to do anything," I'd retort. The most I could do was to pray for God's mercy as I clung to my Divine Mercy image.

It was God's mercy that I happened across an article that identified lukewarmness as the chronic sadness or discouragement that comes upon a person who laments all the effort that is necessary to live the Christian life. The statement hit me right between the eyes. That was me—lamenting my hurt, nurturing my sadness, and resisting the hard work necessary to truly forgive. God was inviting me to place myself in his hands, forgive my husband, and get on with life. I decided to refuse no longer.

I won't deny it's been a struggle. I was so deeply hurt that it is still sometimes hard to say, "I forgive." Yet with every Our Father I say, especially at Mass, God draws me closer to himself and helps me to renew my decision.

What I have come to see is that my husband and I are both recipients of God's unconditional mercy. In our bedroom hangs a reminder of this reality—a large painting of Jesus, the Divine Mercy. Commissioned from that little image I kept in the laundry room, it now comforts and encourages us both.

Act!

Look back to the beginning of the Reflect! section. Decide to take action to repair a personal relationship. Ask the Holy Spirit to guide you. You can also ask for Judah and Joseph to intercede for you, since the holy men and women of Old Testament times are saints too, even though we don't usually give them that title.

▶ In the Spotlight
Ransoming Captives

Judah asked to take his brother Benjamin's place in slavery. In the history of the Church, there is a tradition of people redeeming others by taking their place in captivity.

In the thirteenth century, Christians in Europe and Muslims in North Africa both took captives in war. People on each side would attempt to ransom their own from captivity. A particular motive for Christians to redeem captives was the danger captivity presented to their faith. By embracing Islam, Christians enslaved in Muslim lands could gain release and become free members of the societies where they were held.

As a young man, Peter Nolasco, a merchant from Barcelona, sometimes acted as a go-between for those wishing to ransom Christian captives from Muslim rulers in Algeria and Tunisia. Around 1200, when he was in his early twenties, Peter decided to devote his life to this work. With some other young men, he gave his property to fund the redemption of captives. One report described the group as laymen who "had a great devotion to Christ who redeemed us by his precious blood."

As the number of captives needing release rose, Peter prayed for guidance. One night in 1218, the Blessed Virgin appeared to him and encouraged him "to transform his group of lay redeemers into a redemptive religious order." With Church approval he organized the Order of the Blessed Virgin Mary of Mercy.

According to the group's founding document, their purpose was "to visit and to free Christians who are in captivity. . . . By this work of mercy . . . all the brothers of this order, as sons of true obedience, must always be gladly disposed to give up their lives, if it is necessary, as Jesus Christ gave up his for us."

The Mercedarians, as they became known—from the Latin word for "mercy"—were crusaders without a sword. They set off to Muslim nations not to fight but to offer their resources and, if it came down to it, their lives, to ransom Christians. In Spain the brothers traveled around with freed captives soliciting donations. When fund-raising fell short of needs, the order would sell its valuables, such as the gold chalices used at Mass.

In North Africa, when funds for redemption were less than needed, Mercedarians would stay behind as hostages until full payment was delivered. On occasion, the balance did not arrive on time and the hostages were cruelly executed. Yet year after year, men volunteered for the work of redemption with faith and enthusiasm. Women joined the order, not to travel as redeemers, but to pray and raise funds.

The Mercedarians have continued into the twenty-first century. Visit them online at orderofmercy.org.

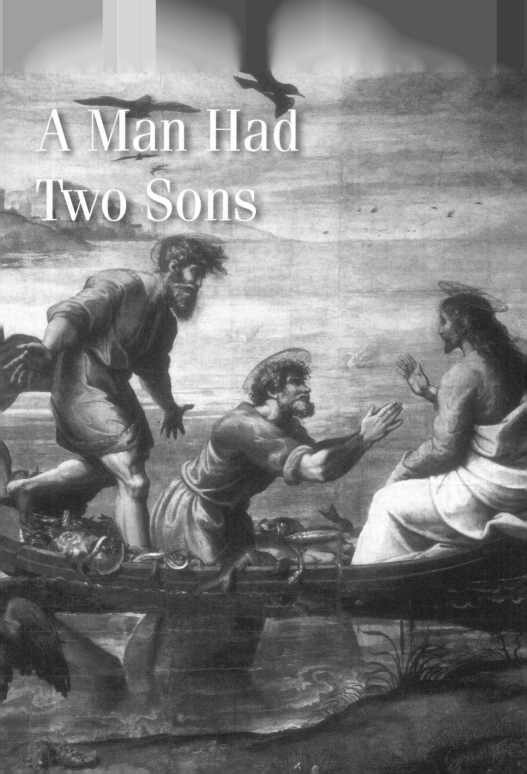

A Man Had Two Sons

Luke 15:1-3, 11-32

15:1Now all the tax collectors and sinners were coming near to listen to him. 2And the Pharisees and the scribes were grumbling and saying, "This fellow welcomes sinners and eats with them." 3So he told them this parable: . . .

11"There was a man who had two sons. 12The younger of them said to his father, 'Father, give me the share of the property that will belong to me.' So he divided his property between them. 13A few days later the younger son gathered all he had and traveled to a distant country, and there he squandered his property in dissolute living. 14When he had spent everything, a severe famine took place throughout that country, and he began to be in need. 15So he went and hired himself out to one of the citizens of that country, who sent him to his fields to feed the pigs. 16He would gladly have filled himself with the pods that the pigs were eating; and no one gave him anything. 17But when he came to himself he said, 'How many of my father's hired hands have bread enough and to spare, but here I am dying of hunger! 18I will get up and go to my father, and I will say to him, "Father, I have sinned against heaven and before you; 19I am no longer worthy to be called your son; treat me like one of your hired hands."' 20So he set off and went to his father. But while he was still far off, his father saw him and was filled with compassion; he ran and put his arms around him and kissed him. 21Then the son said to him, 'Father, I have sinned against heaven and before you; I am no longer worthy to be called your son.' 22But the father said to his slaves, 'Quickly, bring out a robe—the best one—and put it on him; put a ring on his finger and sandals on his feet. 23And get the fatted calf and

Go your way; as you live, it cannot be that the son of these tears should perish."
—A bishop to the mother of St. Augustine as she prayed for his conversion. From Augustine's *Confessions*

kill it, and let us eat and celebrate; ²⁴for this son of mine was dead and is alive again; he was lost and is found!' And they began to celebrate.

²⁵"Now his elder son was in the field; and when he came and approached the house, he heard music and dancing. ²⁶He called one of the slaves and asked what was going on. ²⁷He replied, 'Your brother has come, and your father has killed the fatted calf, because he has got him back safe and sound.' ²⁸Then he became angry and refused to go in. His father came out and began to plead with him. ²⁹But he answered his father, 'Listen! For all these years I have been working like a slave for you, and I have never disobeyed your command; yet you have never given me even a young goat so that I might celebrate with my friends. ³⁰But when this son of yours came back, who has devoured your property with prostitutes, you killed the fatted calf for him!' ³¹Then the father said to him, 'Son, you are always with me, and all that is mine is yours. ³²But we had to celebrate and rejoice, because this brother of yours was dead and has come to life; he was lost and has been found.'"

A young man bursts out of his house and strides up a narrow cobblestone street. Passing the last of his village's low stone buildings, he heads out into the countryside, to an area of sloping fields and terraced farms, and then stops to look around. This is his family's property.

The man gazes at an orchard of silvery olive trees and a recently harvested wheat field where goats are grazing in the stubble. Cows are standing in a meadow beyond. "Who *cares* about all of this?" he says to himself. "This place is a chain around my neck."

Back at the house, a confrontation ensues. "Dad, this place is closing in on me! I've got to get out. I can't stand another day here. Give me my inheritance now." It is not much of a conversation, just a series of "me" statements with an unspoken "wish you were dead" at the end. "All right," his father says.

A portion of the chain is sold and the proceeds are put in the young man's hands. There is no extended leave-taking ("I am *so* out of here!"). The plan is simply to get far away and have a really good time. After that, who knows? Prudence and her solemn-faced sisters Patience and Delayed-Gratification are not the kind of gals the young man is aiming to hang out with.

So nothing unusual here—except, perhaps, the absence of any pushback from the father. The interesting question is not whether the young man's adventure in reality denial will crash and burn, but what he will do if he manages to stagger from the wreckage.

> He doesn't envision reconciliation with his dad. Does he even want it?

As it happens, our hero hits bottom at a pigsty. (Can a Jewish boy sink lower?) Sitting there hungry, watching well-fed hogs wallow in the mud, he comes to his senses. "If I stay here, I'm going to die. I'd better go home and ask for a job on the family farm."

Absent from the young man's thoughts, it seems, are reflections on the pain he has caused his father. He does intend to admit that he *has* sinned against him. But the little speech he composes sounds less like a confession than a cover sheet to his job application. He doesn't envision reconciliation with his dad. Does he even want it? What, clearly, he wants is to avoid starving to death.

Is this repentance? Biblical scholar Arland Hultgren suggests it is "a prelude to repentance, even if not repentance itself." But now we come to the real surprise in this story: the answer the father gives to this question.

A mild man but a realist, the father had a pretty good idea how quickly his son would burn through the accumulated profits of generations jingling in his money purse. It was also easy to envision the endgame: without friends or family in a foreign country. As his son left, the father gave him up for dead.

And yet, lo and behold, here he is, walking into the village! From the sight of him, the father knows instantly that it is desperate need that has driven him to return. But he will take his son as he is. Far from scrutinizing his son's repentance speech for signs of genuineness, the father cuts it short. His son has come home alive; that is enough. Enough? It is *everything*!

The son's return is so wonderful that his rehabilitation cannot be delayed even the few minutes it would take to get everyone into the house. He must be reinstated right there in the street, with the neighbors watching—the neighbors who know all about how disgracefully the young man has acted. And then celebration is not only appropriate but urgent. The party must begin before anyone thinks to send word to the older brother, who is laboring out on the property.

Ah, Older Brother. He is out on the hillside, cultivating what is left of the wheat field and tending the goats, doing the work from which young "bro" went AWOL. Unsummoned, he eventually completes his chores and returns to find the house in an uproar.

Like Dad, Older Brother too had given up Younger Brother for dead. Unlike Dad, he is not pleased by his unexpected resurrection. But what really steams him is that Dad is treating the refugee from the pigsty as though he has come back from a military deployment wearing a Bronze Star.

As far as Older Brother is concerned, Younger Brother should have stayed dead. He has nothing to say to him. He does, however, have some choice words for Dad, when the older man again humiliates himself by going out into the street to transact family business.

"Look, Dad, *your younger son* is no good. Period."

Unlike an earlier father-son conversation, this time the father pushes back. "He's *your brother*. And he's come back from the dead. How could we not celebrate?"

There the story ends, and we realize that it is not so much about a prodigal son as about a father who has two sons. He loves both of them extravagantly and shamelessly, but neither of them appreciates— or even perceives—his love. Yet when either of them responds in *any* way to his love, the father is overjoyed. And when they do not respond, he keeps trying to show them.

That, Jesus says, is how God is with us.

Understand!

1. Reread Luke 15:1-3. From Jesus' story about the father and two sons, what can we infer about what was going on with the tax collectors and other prominent sinners that he was socializing with?

   _____

   _____

   _____

   _____

   _____

   _____

2. How might the younger son's relationship with his father be different after his return from before he left? After the welcome home party, what issues in their relationship will father and son have to deal with?

_____

_____

_____

_____

_____

3. What picture of the father is reflected in the older son's description of how his father has related to him (Luke 15:29)? In what way does this picture of the father diverge from the picture one gets of him from his responses to his younger son (verses 12, 20-23) and from his words to the older son (verses 31-32)? How would you explain the discrepancy?

_____

_____

_____

_____

_____

4. Compare Jesus' statement about the younger son's activities in Luke 15:13 with what the older son says in verse 30. Again, how would you explain the difference?

_____

_____

_____

_____

_____

5. The route by which Younger Son comes to a change of heart is his experience of the consequences of his bad decisions. What might be the older son's route to a change of heart? What, exactly, is the change of heart that the older son needs?

_____

_____

_____

_____

_____

_____

▶ In the Spotlight
An Ill-Advised Transaction?

We might wonder whether the younger son's request for his inheritance was an accepted thing to do in the ancient Near East. According to New Testament scholar Arland Hultgren, "There is no known evidence of law or custom to suggest that it was a normal procedure to pass on one's property while still alive, nor for the potential heir to ask for it, although it would not be inconceivable for a parent to initiate such a course of action. Otherwise it would be impossible to account for the saying in Sirach 33:20-22." The instruction in the Book of Sirach that Hultgren refers to is this:

To son or wife, to brother or friend,
    do not give power over yourself, as long as you live;
and do not give your property to another,
    in case you change your mind and must ask for it.
While you are still alive and have breath in you,
    do not let anyone take your place.
For it is better that your children should ask from you

than that you should look to the hand of your children."
(33:20-22)

Sirach adds:

At the time when you end the days of your life,
    in the hour of death, distribute your inheritance.
(33:24)

Therefore, Hultgren continues, "The request of the younger son . . . is exceedingly brash, even insolent. It is tantamount to wishing that the father were dead! Moreover, by leaving his father, he cast aside his obligation to care for him in old age. He rejected the duty of a son to honor his father and mother, as spelled out in the Decalogue (Exodus 20:12; Deuteronomy 5:16). That lot fell to the older son alone."

The father in the parable, then, does not follow custom in giving his younger son his share of the inheritance while he is still alive. What might have led him to take this seemingly unwise course of action?

Grow!

1. When did a painful experience help you to see that you needed to change something in your life? How did you respond? From this, can you learn something for dealing with a particular area of your life now?

_____

_____

_____

_____

_____

_____

2. The younger son's return home may not have been based on deep repentance, but it was a step in the right direction. Is there a situation in your life in which you have taken a first step but need to go further?

_____

_____

_____

_____

_____

_____

3. Neither of this man's sons seems to think of him as _father_. When do you think of God as _your_ Father? (Do you think of him as your Father?) What impact does knowing God as Father make on how you live?

_____

_____

_____

_____

_____

_____

4. Do you sympathize with the older brother? Is his protest to his father similar to thoughts you have had regarding God's relationship with you? If so, what message for yourself do you hear in this story?

_____

_____

_____

_____

_____

_____

5. The father went out to each of his sons regardless of what people might think of him. When do considerations of how people might think of you interfere with your extending forgiveness and being reconciled with someone?

_____

_____

_____

_____

_____

_____

▶ In the Spotlight
When a Child Needs to Forgive theParent

Gretchen Traylor was only three pounds at birth, and her mother, a single woman, abandoned her at the hospital. Gretchen was adopted by loving parents, but her undeveloped lungs had already suffered permanent damage. During childhood, she experienced constant respiratory illnesses. Nevertheless, she studied hard, became a high school teacher, married, and became an adoptive parent. In middle age, however, her health deteriorated and she faced the need of a lung transplant, which would end her teaching career.

Knowing that her birth mother had not gotten prenatal care and had abandoned her, Gretchen began to feel an intense anger against her, blaming her for her ill health. "I knew I was doing wrong and prayed for forgiveness. At the same time, I held on to my hatred with both hands, justifying myself to God: 'She's to blame for all my problems!'

"During this time, my son was preparing for Confirmation. We were expected at church for a special Mass before his reception of the sacrament. I was sick but rose and went, coughing and grumbling to myself all the way: 'I don't want to go. What good is Confirmation anyway? How is it helping me now?' By the time I entered the pew, I felt thoroughly enraged.

"Then Father came out and began addressing the Confirmation class: 'Young people, you are about to receive a gift so precious that it is nearly beyond words to describe.' He told them that the Holy Spirit would, if asked, heal all hurts, provide all gifts, build up all strength, guide all paths, and make all things new, no matter what the circumstances.

"It was as if a light went on. Realizing that no one else could help me, I found myself begging God for a renewal of the Spirit in my soul. 'Lord,' I prayed, 'even though I know my rage is harming me, even though I know you forgive us and tell us to forgive others, I just can't forgive my birth mother on my own. I need you to do it in me, Lord. Please!'

"Immediately, I heard these words within my heart: *I know your struggles. And I know your heart. Without your illness, you would not be the person you are today. Forgive your mother, for I used your premature birth for my purposes.* As the message ended, I felt something heavy lifting from my shoulders. Then my heart was flooded with such joy that I could only weep and shake with praise and gratitude."

After this, Gretchen's health improved. In the years since, she has led the development of a program in the Archdiocese of St. Paul-Minneapolis to acknowledge the sacrifices of birth mothers who have relinquished their babies to adoption and to offer opportunities for healing.

Reflect!

1. "Return to me, for I have redeemed you" (Isaiah 44:22). God takes the initiative to open the way for us to return to him. Where can

you detect God's grace opening the way for you to repent of some sin or be reconciled with someone you have hurt?

2. The older brother did not like the way his father fell over himself in his eagerness to forgive the younger brother. This displeasure at God's mercy to other people is addressed by Jesus in another parable he tells. Does it lead you to examine your own attitudes to others?

> The kingdom of heaven is like a landowner who went out early in the morning to hire laborers for his vineyard. After agreeing with the laborers for the usual daily wage, he sent them into his vineyard. When he went out about nine o'clock, he saw others standing idle in the marketplace; and he said to them, "You also go into the vineyard, and I will pay you whatever is right." So they went. When he went out again about noon and about three o'clock, he did the same. And about five o'clock he went out and found others standing around; and he said to them, "Why are you standing here idle all day?" They said to him, "Because no one has hired us." He said to them, "You also go into the vineyard." When evening came, the owner of the vineyard said to his manager, "Call the laborers and give them their pay, beginning with the last and then going to the first." When those hired about five o'clock came, each of them received the usual daily wage. Now when the first came, they thought they would receive more; but each of them also received the usual daily wage. And when they received it, they grumbled against the landowner, saying, "These last worked only one hour, and you have made them equal to us who have borne the burden of the day and the scorching heat." But he replied to one of them, "Friend, I am doing you no wrong; did you not agree with me for the usual daily wage? Take what belongs to

you and go; I choose to give to this last the same as I give to you. Am I not allowed to do what I choose with what belongs to me? Or are you envious because I am generous?" So the last will be first, and the first will be last. (Matthew 20:1-16)

▶ In the Spotlight
A French Lieutenant

The prodigal son in Jesus' parable is so called because he was recklessly extravagant. He was no less prodigal than Charles de Foucauld, who inherited a fortune from the grandfather who raised him after his parents' death. As soon as he had finished at the French military academy, in 1880, the new Lieutenant de Foucauld proceeded to go through his wealth at a great rate—entertaining, dining (he was overweight), drinking, gambling, and dressing in expensive attire. He went off in high style to his first assignment, which was in Algeria.

There his military career soon came to an end. The French army expelled him for "notorious misconduct." His crime was impropriety: he insisted on bringing his mistress to social functions as though she were his wife.

Back in France and aimless, Charles realized that his time in Algeria had given him an interest in North Africa. He began to study the languages of the region and then carried out a dangerous exploration of Morocco. This not only produced an award-winning book, but it also brought him into contact with ordinary Moroccan Muslims. He was struck by their faith in God and daily prayer. Charles had drifted away from Catholicism. Now he began to spend hours each day in a nearby church. "My God," he prayed, "if you exist, make your presence known to me." A cousin, Marie, and a priest, Father Huvelin, helped Charles find his way back to God.

Charles wrote, "As soon as I believed that there was a God, I understood that I could not do anything other than live for him." But how? He visited a monastery, and the monks' poverty "won his heart," Marie wrote. At Father Huvelin's suggestion, he made a pilgrimage to the Holy Land. What impressed him there, biographer Robert Ellsberg writes, was that "Jesus, the Son of God, had been a poor man and a worker. As a carpenter in Nazareth, Jesus had, in these lowly circumstances, embodied the gospel message in its entirety, before ever announcing it in words."

After spending some years in several Trappist monasteries, Charles went back to Nazareth and lived as a handyman for a convent of nuns. Returning to France, he was ordained a priest. Then, finally, grasping his vocation, he returned to North Africa and lived among the Tuareg, a people in southern Algeria. There he was a mostly silent witness to God's love, praying, studying the Tuareg's language and poetry, and caring for slaves and children. He shared what he had with his neighbors and welcomed visitors.

Charles was killed in 1916 when a local military unit fighting the French swept through the village where he was living. He died with no accomplishments to show for his quiet, humble witness to Christ. Since his death, however, several religious groups have formed in response to his example, all of them with the words "Little Brothers" or "Little Sisters" in their names.

Act!

What little "pigsty" of sin in your life do you need to depart from? What action do you need to take to get started on your way home to the house of your Father?

▶ In the Spotlight
Praying Like a Prodigal Son—or Daughter

In the Byzantine tradition, the Sunday two weeks before the beginning of Lent is called the Sunday of the Prodigal Son because that parable is the gospel reading. In the run-up to the penitential season, Jesus' parable is a call to self-examination and, even more, to reflection on God's mercy. Among the prayers in that Sunday's liturgy is this one, which also refers to the "Thief" in Luke 23:39-43 and the "Publican" in Luke 18:10-14:

Behold, O Christ, the affliction of my heart; behold my turning back; behold my tears, O Savior, and despise me not. But embrace me once again in your compassion and count me with the multitude of the saved, that with thanksgiving I may sing the praises of your mercy.

As the Thief I cry to you, "Remember me." As the Publican, with eyes cast down to earth, I beat my breast and say, "Be merciful." As the Prodigal deliver me from every evil, O King who pity all, that I may sing the praises of your boundless compassion.

Groan now, my soul, all wretched, and cry aloud to Christ: O Lord who for my sake became poor of your own will, in my poverty I lack every good work: make me rich with the abundance of your blessings, for you alone are full of love and mercy.

O loving Lord, once you rejoiced at the voluntary return of the Prodigal: rejoice now because of me, wretched though I am: open your holy embrace to me, that saved I may sing the praises of your boundless compassion.

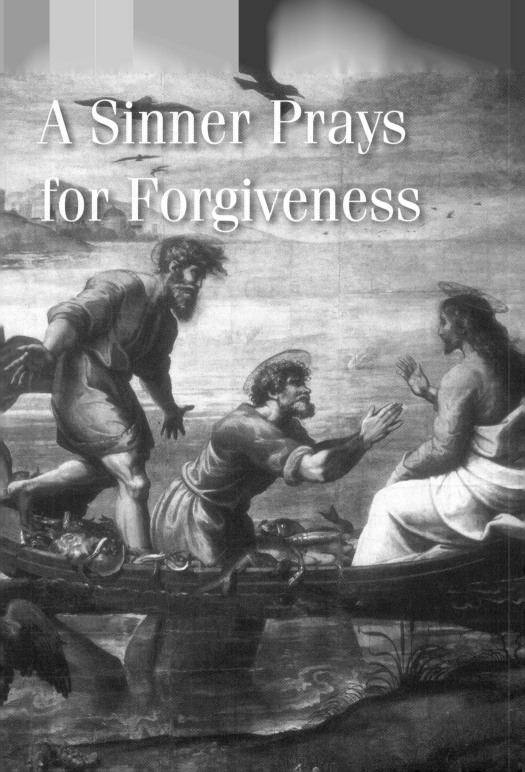

A Sinner Prays for Forgiveness

Psalm 51

To the leader. A Psalm of David, when the prophet Nathan came to him, after he had gone in to Bathsheba.

51:1Have mercy on me, O God, according to your steadfast
    love;
    according to your abundant mercy blot out my
    transgressions.
2Wash me thoroughly from my iniquity,
    and cleanse me from my sin.

3For I know my transgressions,
    and my sin is ever before me.
4Against you, you alone, have I sinned,
    and done what is evil in your sight,
so that you are justified in your sentence
    and blameless when you pass judgment.
5Indeed, I was born guilty,
    a sinner when my mother conceived me.

> Deal with us according to your kindness, O Physician and Healer of our souls.
> —Byzantine prayer on Good Friday

6You desire truth in the inward being;
    therefore teach me wisdom in my secret heart.
7Purge me with hyssop, and I shall be clean;
    wash me, and I shall be whiter than snow.
8Let me hear joy and gladness;
    let the bones that you have crushed rejoice.
9Hide your face from my sins,
    and blot out all my iniquities.

10Create in me a clean heart, O God,
    and put a new and right spirit within me.

¹¹Do not cast me away from your presence,
    and do not take your holy spirit from me.
¹²Restore to me the joy of your salvation,
    and sustain in me a willing spirit.

¹³Then I will teach transgressors your ways,
    and sinners will return to you.
¹⁴Deliver me from bloodshed, O God, O God of my salvation,
    and my tongue will sing aloud of your deliverance.

¹⁵O Lord, open my lips,
    and my mouth will declare your praise.
¹⁶For you have no delight in sacrifice;
    if I were to give a burnt offering, you would not be pleased.
¹⁷The sacrifice acceptable to God is a broken spirit;
    a broken and contrite heart, O God, you will not despise.

¹⁸Do good to Zion in your good pleasure;
    rebuild the walls of Jerusalem,
¹⁹then you will delight in right sacrifices,
    in burnt offerings and whole burnt offerings;
    then bulls will be offered on your altar.

"I had an affair with his wife."

"How well did you know him?"

"He was under my command—one of the bravest men I ever met. And that's how I got rid of him. I planned an engagement just for him—an attack on an enemy position that was sure to go bad. I knew he'd hold his ground. He didn't disappoint."

"After he died?"

"I married his wife."

That, briefly, is the story behind the introductory line above verse 1 of Psalm 51. After an adulterous liaison with the wife of one of his military officers, David designed a hopeless assault on an enemy position to get rid of him. You can read the account of David, Bathsheba, and Uriah in 2 Samuel 12.

In the hundreds of pages between Cain's murder of Abel and Judas's betrayal of Jesus, no crime stands out as more cold-blooded. By connecting Psalm 51 with it, the biblical editor marked this prayer as an expression of repentance from very grave sin. No matter how great your sin or mine may be, this prayer is spacious enough to accommodate it.

> No matter how great your sin or mine may be, this prayer is spacious enough to accommodate it.

In our readings about Judah, Joseph, and the prodigal son, we observed a change of heart from the outside. Now we get a look inside the experience, in the form of a prayer. We are invited to pray this prayer ourselves, to share in the psalmist's awareness of sin and his crying out to the Lord. It is not, however, an easy invitation to accept. The psalmist is tormented by guilt. If the younger son experienced the breeze of repentance, this psalmist feels its full gale force. The young man decided to own up to his sin so that he could get a job and stay alive. The psalmist wants to be unburdened of his sin because it is crushing the life out of him. Unlike many of those whose voices we hear in psalms of appeal, he is not seeking physical healing or vindication against enemies. Release from guilt is the thing he is seeking, the thing for which he feels a desperate need.

His sin is always with him (Psalm 51:3). He can't get it out of his mind. What most oppresses him is not the thought that he has hurt someone or has fallen short of his own expectations for himself, but that he has offended God. "Against you, you alone, have I sinned" (verse 4); this is his deepest sorrow.

We might think that the more clearly the psalmist looks at his sin as an offense against God, the more desperate he would feel: his consciousness of the contrast between God's rightness and his own wrongness would lead him to despair. Yet the result is just the opposite. The more frankly the psalmist acknowledges God's righteousness ("You are justified in your sentence / and blameless when you pass judgment"—verse 4), the more confident he becomes that God does not simply reward the obedient and punish the disobedient. He senses that God's righteousness encompasses a determination to overcome evil, a desire to set things right in us, to straighten out everything that is twisted out of shape in our lives. As the psalmist honestly confesses his sin, then, his trust in God's desire to save him grows. And that, obviously, is the only thing he *can* trust in, given his moral failure and violation of his relationship with God.

The psalmist also senses that his recognition of his sin, tormenting though it may be, stems from God's action in him. The reason he has come to know his transgressions is that God "causes him to know wisdom in his secret heart" (an alternate way of translating verse 6). "I wouldn't recognize what a sinner I am unless you were helping me to see it," the psalmist is saying. His feelings of guilt are God's voice speaking to him in his conscience, prodding him to face up to his sin so that he can be freed of it. Thus, the psalmist's anguish is, in a strange way, a sign of God's presence; like feeling a dentist's drill grinding away at a decayed portion of a tooth, it is no cause for despair. So the psalmist calls out vigorously to God. "Put me through the laundry! Bleach out my sins!" (see verse 7). "Remove the guilt that is crushing me, and save me from the mess I've made of myself!"

The first part of the psalm (verses 1-9) looks back to past misdeeds and is filled with words for sin. In the second part, words for sin virtually disappear, replaced by words for God as the psalmist thinks about the future (verses 10-19). Experience has demonstrated how deeply flawed he is. As long as he can remember, he has always had unruly tendencies to do what is wrong (verse 5). Remorse, by itself, will not be enough to ensure that he will do better in the future. He needs an eager attentiveness to God's voice, a desire for what is right that overcomes his desires for what is wrong—and a power in his will to actually *choose* what is right. The psalmist needs a fundamental change, and that is beyond him. Indeed, a fundamental change seems impossible. But that is exactly what he seeks from God: "Create in me a clean heart" (verse 10).

At the end, the psalmist acknowledges that offering an animal sacrifice in the temple would at this moment be inappropriate. The sacrificial system was not set up to provide atonement for deliberate serious sins. Forgiveness is not something we can buy from God by offering a goat or giving money or doing good deeds. Forgiveness—and a change of heart—are God's gifts, which he gives freely to those who appeal to his mercy.

Understand!

1. What reasons does the psalmist offer to God for why God should forgive him and transform him?

2. Reread verse 2. Since the psalmist has been unfaithful to God, how can he expect God to be faithful to him?

_____

_____

_____

_____

_____

_____

3. Since most sins involve other people, why does the psalmist say to God, "Against you, you alone, have I sinned" (verse 4)?

_____

_____

_____

_____

_____

_____

4. What does it mean to *offer* God a "broken and contrite heart" (verse 17)?

_____

_____

_____

_____

_____

_____

5. How does prayer for God's people (verses 18-19) fit into an individual's psalm of repentance?

_____

_____

_____

_____

_____

_____

▶ In the Spotlight
Asking Too Much?

"Let me hear joy and gladness" (Psalm 51:8). One might wonder if the psalmist is not overreaching here. Joy seems more than he should expect, given the gravity of his sins. Shouldn't he limit himself to asking for forgiveness? Imagine a person who has fallen behind in his mortgage payments going to the bank and trying to work out an extended payment plan—and then asking for the one hundred dollar gift card offered to people who open a new checking account!

St. Robert Bellarmine explains the psalmist's prayer for joy this way. It is as though the sinner is saying to God, "When you've washed me completely, I know you will add this kindness, that in some wonderful way you will give me joy as a sign that my sins are forgiven—a joy that will be like a trustworthy messenger, to which I will gladly listen with the ear of my heart."

Probably many of us would say that this joy of knowing we are forgiven is one of the most mysterious and powerful effects of receiving the Sacrament of Reconciliation.

Grow!

1. What experience of guilt in your life comes closest to that of the psalmist in this prayer? Has this guilt been resolved by seeking God's forgiveness? Is there anyone else's forgiveness you need to seek?

_____

_____

_____

_____

_____

_____

2. Judging from this prayer, what would you say about the experience of guilt? How might it bear fruit in someone's life? How might it be negative or unhelpful?

_____

_____

_____

_____

_____

3. In what situations do you find it difficult to make a straightforward acknowledgment of sin, as the psalmist does in verse 4?

_____

_____

_____

_____

_____

4. In verse 4, the psalmist acknowledges that he is in the wrong and God is in the right. Thus, the psalmist will not make any excuses for his sins. ("I only did it once." "I didn't think it would have such bad consequences.") He won't blame God in any way. ("You gave me a hard childhood." "You let hard temptations come my way.") Nor will he complain about God's moral standards. ("You expect too much." "Your ideas of right and wrong don't make sense in the real world.") What excuses or complaints do you tend to make to God regarding your sins?

_____

_____

_____

_____

_____

_____

5. The psalmist pleads with God for his presence, power, Spirit, joy, and salvation (verses 10-12). What experiences of struggle against sin have impressed on you your need for God? What implications does this recognition have for how you should live today?

_____

_____

_____

_____

_____

_____

▶ In the Spotlight
How Clean Is Clean Enough?

Franciscan Father Dave Pivonka walked the centuries-old pilgrimage trail through northern Spain to the shrine of St. James and wrote about his experience in a book called *Hiking the Camino*. In it he describes how pilgrims on the trail washed their clothes each afternoon at the end of the day's hike. Usually there was just a basin of cold water at the lodgings. Given the primitive facilities, Father Dave's efforts at laundry were minimal. But he noticed that some of the women put a *lot* of effort into the task—scrubbing and rinsing, repeating the process more than once, scrutinizing their work to make sure all soil was removed, then hanging everything up neatly to dry. Here he explains his reaction:

> They washed to get their clothes clean. . . . I only wanted to make sure my clothes didn't stink.
>
> This led to a startling thought. I realized that a lot of the time when I repent for my sin and go to confession, it is not because I truly want to be clean; rather it is because I don't want to "stink" any more. I don't want to feel guilty or feel bad.
>
> Sadly, I fear, I have often gone to confession as a "quick rinse cycle." I go before God, repent of my sin and in some way feel as if I have done what is expected of me. But oftentimes, if I were to be totally honest with myself, I did not go to confession so that I would be clean or pure but just so that I could stand myself. . . . It is the difference between "Bless me, Father, for I did x, y, and z" and "Bless me, Father, for I have broken God's heart."
>
> There is a profound difference between approaching God because *I* feel bad or guilty and going before the one whom I have offended, the one who loves me perfectly,

and saying I am sorry for breaking his heart. In the one case I am at the center; in the other it is God.

Don't get me wrong: It is always good to repent before God. This is never a bad thing, but there is more. I believe one type of repentance is motivated by love, and the other by guilt, fear, superstition, or any number of things. . . .

I hope that I never use the confessional as a "quick wash" cycle, without remembering what Jesus did that allowed me to be forgiven. . . . I pray that, when I go to confession, I am motivated to be pure and clean, the same way some of my fellow pilgrims were motivated to actually wash their clothes.

Reflect!

1. What does the psalmist mean by "a broken spirit" (51:17)? What part does it play in the process of repentance? Old Testament scholar Artur Weiser writes about a broken spirit, or "contrite heart": "We should be mistaken if we were to interpret the phrase of a contrite heart as reflecting only the poet's momentary state of mind . . . for these words are spoken with a view to the thanksgiving that will *follow* the forgiveness of sins and therefore characterize the basic attitude which man is to observe in all circumstances." In other words, the psalmist does not expect this condition to go away but to become permanent. In what way should a broken or contrite heart be a continuing part of our lives? On this, consider Matthew 5:4.

2. The psalmist says, "I was born guilty, / a sinner when my mother conceived me" (51:5). Compare this statement to God's observation that "the inclination of the human heart is evil from youth" (Genesis 8:21). And on the issue of human depravity, consider also 1 Kings 8:46; Job 4:17; 14:4; 15:14-15; 25:4; Psalms 143:2;

Proverbs 20:9. Obviously, these statements do not express everything about us as human beings. What truth do they express? How have you experienced it?

3. Ponder God's promises of a new heart and spirit:

> I will give them a heart to know that I am the LORD; and they shall be my people and I will be their God, for they shall return to me with their whole heart. (Jeremiah 24:7)

> But this is the covenant that I will make with the house of Israel after those days, says the LORD: I will put my law within them, and I will write it on their hearts; and I will be their God, and they shall be my people. No longer shall they teach one another, or say to each other, "Know the LORD," for they shall all know me, from the least of them to the greatest, says the LORD; for I will forgive their iniquity, and remember their sin no more. (Jeremiah 31:33-34)

> I will give them one heart and one way, that they may fear me for all time, for their own good and the good of their children after them. I will make an everlasting covenant with them, never to draw back from doing good to them; and I will put the fear of me in their hearts, so that they may not turn from me. (Jeremiah 32:39-40)

> I will sprinkle clean water upon you, and you shall be clean from all your uncleannesses, and from all your idols I will cleanse you. A new heart I will give you, and a new spirit I will put within you; and I will remove from your body the heart of stone and give you a heart of flesh. I will put my spirit within you, and make you follow my statutes and be careful to observe my ordinances. (Ezekiel 36:25-27)

4. Ponder St. Paul on our being a new creation in Jesus Christ:

> So if anyone is in Christ, there is a new creation: everything old has passed away; see, everything has become new! (2 Corinthians 5:17)

> For neither circumcision nor uncircumcision is anything; but a new creation is everything! (Galatians 6:15)

> He has abolished the law with its commandments and ordinances, that he might create in himself one new humanity in place of the two, thus making peace. (Ephesians 2:15)

▶ In the Spotlight
Accepting the Grace of Confession

Francis Ford Coppola's three *Godfather* movies tell the story of Michael Corleone, the son of a man who built a crime family in New York City. By the end of the first film, young Michael has inherited his father's place at the head of the family. At the beginning of the third film, after a career involving murder after murder, Michael is in his sixties and hoping to exit from the world of crime. Halfway through this film, Michael gets into a business conversation with Cardinal Lamberto, who senses the burden of guilt he carries.

"Would you like to make your confession?" the churchman asks unexpectedly.

Caught off guard, Michael deflects the suggestion with some meaningless excuses. Besides, he says, "I'm beyond redemption."

"Sometimes," Lamberto responds, "the desire to confess is overwhelming, and we must seize the moment."

After a further protest—"What is the point of confessing if I don't repent?"—Michael makes a brief but honest confession. His most grievous sin: the murder of his brother. After acknowledging it, he breaks down and weeps.

The cardinal watches and listens. Then he tells Michael, "Your sins are terrible. And it is just that you suffer. Your life could be redeemed, but I know you don't believe that. You will not change."

Afterwards, Michael seems in better spirits. But soon he is drawn again into the vortex of murder and revenge. He expresses the hope that this final crime will be the final act by which he redeems himself and breaks with sin, but his plans end in disaster. Lamberto, it turns out, was right.

This is not surprising. After heading a crime family for decades, it would be unimaginably difficult for Michael to get free of his criminal life. Yet Lamberto must have known that before inviting him to make his confession. Why, then, did the cardinal urge him to it?

Perhaps Lamberto sensed that God was offering Michael the grace to break out of the darkness he had gotten himself into. It was that grace that was to be seized in "the moment." But as Michael made his confession, Lamberto realized that he was not taking hold of the grace God was offering. "Your life could be redeemed," the cardinal said, "but I know you don't believe that."

Thus, the scene in *The Godfather Part III*, fictional though it may be, exposes the central reality of the Sacrament of Confession: God offers to restore in us what, humanly speaking, is beyond redemption. And this highlights the central issue: are we willing not only to acknowledge our sins but also to accept that grace?

Act!

When we are seeking God's forgiveness, the privileged place for our encounter with him is the Sacrament of Reconciliation. In Confession we not only hear the words of absolution, knowing that we have received God's forgiveness, but we also make contact with Jesus. By his presence in the sacrament, he not only forgives us, but he also strengthens us. And he not only strengthens us, but he continues the process of transforming us that was begun when we were baptized. So plan to go to Confession before you finish this Bible study.

▶ In the Spotlight
Setting Things Right

"Against you, you alone, have I sinned," the psalmist tells God (Psalm 51:4). Does he mean literally that he has not sinned against anyone else but God? Perhaps, for it is possible to sin against God alone. But it seems more likely that the psalmist's declaration is a way of saying that in sinning against other people, the person he most offended was God.

The psalmist, then, needs to seek forgiveness not only from God but also from whomever he has hurt. And seeking reconciliation will involve restitution. How can I expect the person I have hurt to forgive me if I am not willing to make good the harm I have done?

The *Catechism of the Catholic Church* is simple and straightforward. "Many sins wrong our neighbor. One must do what is possible in order to repair the harm (e.g., return stolen goods, restore the reputation of someone slandered, pay compensation for injuries). Simple justice requires as much" (1459).

Sadly, with the passage of time, some injustices cannot be remedied. But where it is possible to do something to ameliorate the damage we have done to our neighbor, the Old Testament offers a useful pointer. In cases of fraud, the rule was that the guilty party should not only "repay the principal amount" to the owner but also "add one-fifth to it" (Leviticus 6:5). In other words, if I've failed in my obligations to someone, I shouldn't only make up for what I haven't done. I should do something extra.

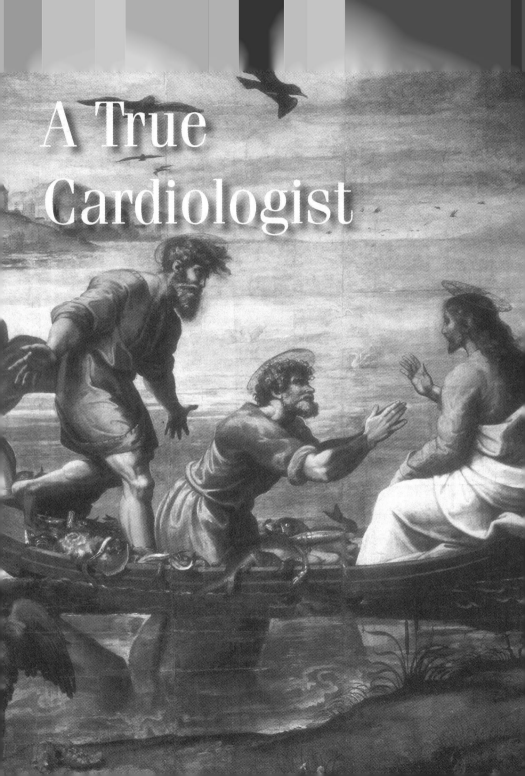

A True
Cardiologist

Matthew 5:21-30, 38-48

5:21 "You have heard that it was said to those of ancient times, 'You shall not murder'; and 'whoever murders shall be liable to judgment.' 22But I say to you that if you are angry with a brother or sister, you will be liable to judgment; and if you insult a brother or sister, you will be liable to the council; and if you say, 'You fool,' you will be liable to the hell of fire. 23So when you are offering your gift at the altar, if you remember that your brother or sister has something against you, 24leave your gift there before the altar and go; first be reconciled to your brother or sister, and then come and offer your gift. 25Come to terms quickly with your accuser while you are on the way to court with him, or your accuser may hand you over to the judge, and the judge to the guard, and you will be thrown into prison. 26Truly I tell you, you will never get out until you have paid the last penny.

> I see the church as a field hospital.
> —Pope Francis

27"You have heard that it was said, 'You shall not commit adultery.' 28But I say to you that everyone who looks at a woman with lust has already committed adultery with her in his heart. 29If your right eye causes you to sin, tear it out and throw it away; it is better for you to lose one of your members than for your whole body to be thrown into hell. 30And if your right hand causes you to sin, cut it off and throw it away; it is better for you to lose one of your members than for your whole body to go into hell. . . .

38"You have heard that it was said, 'An eye for an eye and a tooth for a tooth.' 39But I say to you, Do not resist an evildoer. But if anyone strikes you on the right cheek, turn the other also; 40and if anyone wants to sue you and take your coat, give your cloak as well; 41and if anyone forces you to go one mile, go also the second mile. 42Give to everyone who begs from you, and do not refuse anyone who wants to borrow from you.

⁴³"You have heard that it was said, 'You shall love your neighbor and hate your enemy.' ⁴⁴But I say to you, Love your enemies and pray for those who persecute you, ⁴⁵so that you may be children of your Father in heaven; for he makes his sun rise on the evil and on the good, and sends rain on the righteous and on the unrighteous. ⁴⁶For if you love those who love you, what reward do you have? Do not even the tax collectors do the same? ⁴⁷And if you greet only your brothers and sisters, what more are you doing than others? Do not even the Gentiles do the same? ⁴⁸Be perfect, therefore, as your heavenly Father is perfect."

Here we have Jesus' great call to a change of heart—the Sermon on the Mount. Let's examine his instructions and then consider our response.

Verses 21-26. Jesus clarifies a number of Old Testament commands. The first concerns killing. Jesus shows that the commandment against killing was not given just to define murder as a crime; the intention of the command is to point us toward true righteousness in relationships, which involves more than avoiding murder. The command directs our attention to the inner turmoil that leads to violence—the kind of anger that makes us want to hurt the other person. If we agree to that kind of anger, we commit a bit of murder in our hearts, Jesus says, even if our outward behavior is mild in comparison (maybe we just say something insulting). So we should deal with murder at its root, repudiating the desire to see the other person suffer. True rightness begins in the heart, in what we intend toward the other person. And it continues outward, seeking reconciliation when a break in the relationship has occurred.

Verses 27-30. Similarly, the commandment against adultery is not just a constraint on behavior. By prohibiting adultery (and, by implication, all sexual intimacy outside marriage), the command directs our attention to the importance of right relationships between men and women. When men have their sexual desires under control, their relationships with women can be wholesome rather than exploitative. Jesus traces a process: a man looks at a woman as an object of sexual desire and then says an inner yes to the desire. Although Jesus addresses men here, his teaching applies to women as well. If we are committed to loving our neighbor as ourselves (Matthew 7:12), we will hit the escape button as soon as lustful thoughts appear on our mental screen. Jesus uses an even stronger metaphor to describe what our reaction should be to such thoughts and desires.

Verses 38-42. The command for retribution sounds harsh—"an eye for an eye and a tooth for a tooth"—but in the courtroom it serves a purpose. By scaling the punishment to the crime, it prevents excessive penalties. Moreover, as St. Augustine pointed out, imposing retribution only equal to the harm the wrongdoer has

> True rightness begins in the heart, in what we intend toward the other person.

inflicted is a step toward mercy, since the person who initiates the wrongdoing deserves to suffer greater negative consequences than the suffering that he inflicted on the victim. But while the underlying aim of the command is to move us toward justice and peace in our relationships with each other, even equal retaliation may provoke a further reaction. Then where will harm and counter-harm end? Let the cycle end with yourself, Jesus says. Set aside the desire for retribution. New Testament scholar Hans Dieter Betz writes that Jesus calls us to "see nonretaliation as a weapon to combat evil and to help justice prevail."

Verses 43-48. Do good to those who do good to you, evil to those who do evil. What could be more obvious than that? It seems like common sense; to do otherwise would be dishonorable, cowardly, and foolish. Granted, Scripture teaches us to love our neighbors as ourselves

(Leviticus 19:18), but doesn't the neighbor who attacks us lose his status as neighbor? No, Jesus declares! Remember the parable of the Good Samaritan (Luke 10:25-37)? All men and women, *even our enemies*, are our neighbors. We may need to resist others' wrongdoing for the sake of their victims, but "Love your enemies" always applies.

Nonretaliation invites the enemy to have a change of heart. But Jesus grounds love of the enemy in who God is and how he wants us to be, not in the expectation that the enemy will respond positively to our peaceable attitude. Jesus makes no promise that our love will evoke a loving response. No one knows better than he that love can be rejected.

"Daunting" would be an understatement. Jesus calls us to a total cleanup of the deepest, darkest corners of our hearts and to a reaching out in love to absolutely everyone, even those who have hurt us. He seems to be summoning us to a Himalayan climb, one that transforms us to love without limits. In fact, he says so unambiguously: "Be perfect' (Matthew 5:48), that is, become complete and whole. Can we actually *do* that?

It may help to step back and look at the mountain range into which Jesus wants to lead us. It is, in fact, the beauty of his own life, of his self-giving. In the Gospels, we see him tirelessly teaching crowds of strangers (Matthew 9:36; 14:13-21; Mark 6:31-34) and patiently instructing his obtuse disciples (Mark 4:10-20; 7:17-23; 8:13-21, 31-38). Even on the night before his death, he was not focused on himself. He was so concerned about his friends that he used his last meal as an opportunity to give them a lesson in humble service (John 13). Later that night, he interrupted his own anguished prayer to urge them to pray (Mark 14:32-41). As he was led out to the place of execution, his thoughts were on the people he passed along the way (Luke 23:26-31). Even on the cross, he had only kind words for those who had nailed him up to die (Luke 23:34). How can we not admire Jesus? How can we not feel an aspiration to follow him?

And this is crucial: Jesus is not only teacher and model; he is the physician of the sin-sick heart. Like a doctor pointing out a dark spot on an x-ray, he looks into our depths and says to us, "See, here's the problem" (see Mark 7:14-23). More than a diagnostician, he also heals. His teaching—for example, the Sermon on the Mount—is part of the medicine.

For treatment by this physician, there is no deductible, no co-pay, no charge at all. Everything is covered, paid for by himself. We simply need to put ourselves in his hands. The course of treatment may involve painful therapy. His goal exceeds anything we might aspire to: I might like a little less joint pain; he wants to see me turning cartwheels. That is, Jesus wants us to live from hearts filled with love for God and love for other people. And he can enable us to do it.

Understand!

1. Embracing anger in your heart, Jesus indicates, is a kind of participation in murder (Matthew 5:21-22). Is this true of every kind of anger? Consider Matthew 23:13-35; Mark 3:1-6; John 2:14-17; Ephesians 4:26. What distinguishes different kinds of anger? What moral guidelines apply to anger in its different forms?

---

2. Jesus' instructions about anger and lust are accompanied by warnings (Matthew 5:22, 25-26, 29-30), but not his instructions about nonretaliation and love of enemies. What might be the reason for this? Of these instructions, which might be most difficult to follow?

_____

_____

_____

_____

_____

3. It is better to let go of time, money—even clothing!—Jesus says, in order to open the way for peace in a relationship with another person (Matthew 5:40-42). What else might be put on the list of things that should be set aside to make way for peace and reconciliation with other people?

_____

_____

_____

_____

_____

4. Jesus condemns actually looking at another person in a way that regards them as a sexual object (Matthew 5:28). In what other ways might we view another person as a sexual object, even if we were not in their presence physically (i.e., pornography, fantasizing about a fictitious person, engaging in online sexual conversations)? Why does Jesus' teaching also apply in such situations?

_____

_____

_____

_____

5. In Matthew 5:22, 28, 39, and 44, Jesus gives clarifications of the meaning of Old Testament laws. His approach can be applied to other biblical commands. Give it a try. Take some Old Testament commands (for example, Exodus 20:15; 21:15; 21:16; 21:33-34; 22:6; Leviticus 19:16; 19:32) and apply Jesus' format to them: "You have heard it said that . . . [insert command], but I say to you [complete the statement]."

_____

_____

_____

_____

_____

_____

▶ In the Spotlight
Dealing with Temptations with Jesus' Help

"I say to you that everyone who looks at a woman with lust has already committed adultery with her in his heart" (Matthew 5:28). In his book on Jesus' Sermon on the Mount, St. Augustine raised the question as to the meaning of "looks at a woman with lust." It is not, Augustine thought, the pleasure that a man might experience at the sight of a woman. Rather, "it is the full consent to the pleasure: the forbidden craving is not checked, but, given the opportunity, it would gratify its desire."

As Augustine thought about the difference between (a) experiencing a fleeting pleasure that would lead to a wrong action and (b) welcoming this pleasure, he discerned three steps on the road to sin: a suggestion arises in our mind from something we see or remember, it brings us pleasure, and then—and this is the decisive point—we consent to it.

Augustine says, "To yield consent to a forbidden pleasure is a great sin; and the sin which a person commits in yielding consent is in his heart. If he goes further and puts this into action, his passion appears to be sated and quenched; but later on, when the suggestion is repeated, there is enkindled a more intense pleasure; though this pleasure is still much less formidable than the pleasure that comes when repeated acts have formed a habit. To overcome a habit is most difficult."

Augustine's analysis is realistic about the difficulty of breaking a bad habit of giving in to forbidden pleasure, such as sexual temptations. But he is hopeful. "One will overcome a habit if he does not give up and does not dread a Christian's warfare against it under him who is his leader and helper."

It might sound as though Augustine is simply cheering us on to an exercise of will against sinful desires. But Augustine's emphasis is on "him who is his leader and helper"—Jesus. Augustine compares the threefold process of consenting to sinful thoughts, carrying out a sinful act, and developing a sinful habit as a progression from dying, being carried out to burial, and rotting in the tomb. But Augustine reminds us to recall Jesus' words. To the girl who had died, he said, "Little girl, get up!" (Mark 5:41). To the young man being carried out for burial, he said, "Young man, I say to you, rise!" (Luke 7:14). And to Lazarus, whose body had begun to rot in the tomb, Jesus cried out, "Lazarus, come out!" (John 11:43).

Grow!

1. What implications does Matthew 5:22 have for how we should talk about other people online? For how we talk to ourselves about other drivers when we're driving? For how we refer to politicians?

   _____

   _____

   _____

   _____

   _____

   _____

2. Who comes to your mind when you read Matthew 5:23-24? What should you do to repair your relationship with that person?

   _____

   _____

   _____

   _____

   _____

3. Jesus' words about anger, nonretaliation, and love of enemies are concerned with how we relate to people who are not treating us in a friendly or favorable way. Who are these people in your life? How are you relating to them? What change is Jesus calling you to make?

   _____

   _____

   _____

   _____

   _____

4. The exaggerated images in Matthew 5:29-30 make the point that we should be severe with ourselves, while the images in verses 39-42 teach us to not be severe with others. If you were to take this approach more seriously in your own life, what changes would it lead you to make?

_____

_____

_____

_____

_____

_____

5. In Matthew 5:38-44, Jesus teaches us how to respond to someone who has hurt us. When have you *not* taken that approach when you were hurt by someone? What happened? What can you learn from this experience, for the present and for the future?

_____

_____

_____

_____

_____

_____

▶ In the Spotlight
The Goodness of Sexual Desire

Is Jesus opposed to sexual desire? His teaching in the Sermon on the Mount has been misunderstood that way. His words received a helpful commentary from Pope St. John Paul II. New Testament scholar Mary Healy, in turn, offers an explanation of John Paul's interpretation:

The Pope notes that Christ's words in Matthew 5:27-28 seem at first to be a severe warning against eros or erotic passion. Jesus seems to demand that sexual passion be crushed and destroyed. But this would be a false interpretation.

Eros is part of the interior force that attracts us to all that is good, true, and beautiful. It is an echo of God, who is the supreme Goodness, Truth, and Beauty. Eros is good; it is part of the way God created us! This includes the mutual attraction between the sexes, which is oriented toward the one-flesh union of husband and wife. God has written into us the gift of communion, the mysterious reality of his image. And he has built into us the desire that leads to the primary expression of that communion: marriage. Thus eros is not to be crushed but transformed. . . .

The real problem is not with eros but with lust, which distorts and cheapens eros by reducing the other person to an object. In a sense the pope is saying that sexual desire that is mere lust is not erotic *enough!* It is a counterfeit of true eros. It sees only the surface and regards the body as a mere object for one's gratification. It fails to recognize the true dignity and preciousness of the human person revealed through the body.

John Paul II is in no way reducing the severity of Christ's words. He *is* saying that in Christ we now have the capacity to become the true masters of our own deep impulses, "like a guardian who watches over a hidden spring." Particularly in the area of relations with the opposite sex, we have to rediscover the spiritual beauty of the human person revealed through the body in its masculinity and femininity. Christ has liberated the human heart, so that we are now able to sift out the gold of the nuptial meaning of the body from all the ugly accretions of lust.

If this high goal seems humanly unattainable, it is. But it *is* possible through life according to the Spirit.

Reflect!

1. In our reading, Jesus targets a variety of issues in our relationships. Which issue is the most important for you to be dealing with right now?

2. In the Sermon on the Mount, Jesus shows that a literalistic carrying out of God's commandments does not bring a person to the rightness in oneself and one's relationships that God intends. An incident in Jesus' life that touches on this issue is found in chapter 10 of the Gospel of Mark. Why did this man need a change of heart in what he loved? How would accepting Jesus' invitation have led him into a process of change?

> As he was setting out on a journey, a man ran up and knelt before him, and asked him, "Good Teacher, what must I do to inherit eternal life?" Jesus said to him, "Why do you call me good? No one is good but God alone. You know the commandments: 'You shall not murder; You shall not commit adultery; You shall not steal; You shall not bear false witness; You shall not defraud; Honor your father and mother.'" He said to him, "Teacher, I have kept all these since my youth." Jesus, looking at him, loved him and said, "You lack one thing; go, sell what you own, and give the money to the poor, and you will have treasure in heaven; then come, follow me." When he heard this, he was shocked and went away grieving, for he had many possessions. (Mark 10:17-22)

3. Read Jesus' reaction to his betrayal and arrest as well as when he is being mocked by the soldiers (Matthew 26:47-56, 67). How does Jesus follow his own teaching from the Sermon on the Mount?

▶ In the Spotlight
Prayer for the Enemy

After putting her five children to sleep in a tent while on a family camping trip in Montana in 1973, Marietta Jaeger Lane gave them each a hug and kiss good night. Seven-year-old Susie climbed out of her sleeping bag to give her mother a special good-night hug. That was the last time Lane ever saw her youngest child. In the morning the family discovered that someone had cut a hole in the side of the children's tent and abducted Susie, whose stuffed animals were left behind on the ground.

Before leaving their Michigan home for the trip, the family had prayed, specifically asking God to bless and protect them. "And then this happened," Lane said. She recalls asking, "Where are you, God? Where are you in this?

"My motherliness made me go screaming after God, and God was there for me, and I came to understand that nobody grieved more about all the terrible things that had happened to Susie; nobody was grieving more about that than God."

Each time she felt rage and anger toward Susie's abductor, God would tell her, "But that's not how I want you to feel."

The police were not able to find Suzie. As the first anniversary of the abduction approached, Lane gave an interview in which she expressed a desire to speak with her daughter's kidnapper. Exactly a year to the minute after Susie's abduction, Lane's phone rang in the middle of the night, waking her from a sound sleep. It was David Meirhofer, Suzie's abductor, who had called to taunt her. "But he wasn't counting on the spiritual journey that I'd been on during the intervening year," Lane said.

Lane spoke with compassion toward Meirhofer, telling him how terrible he must feel to be burdened with the reality of what he had done, and that God loved him. "He backed down and stayed on the phone for about an hour and twenty minutes," Lane said. "At one point I told him that I had been praying for him, and I asked him what I could do to help him, and he just broke down and said, 'I wish this burden could be lifted from me.'

"He just relaxed and said a lot of things that he probably never in his wildest dreams intended to say, but he gave out enough information about himself that the FBI was able to identify him."

After his arrest, Meirhofer agreed to plead guilty to Susie's murder and to three other murders. He was suspected in as many as a dozen Montana murders. Meirhofer committed suicide the same day of his guilty plea.

Today Lane speaks of her journey as being part of "Susie's parable." Jesus used parables, and the way Lane sees it, God is using her to be a living example of what's possible when it comes to forgiveness and reconciliation.

In the years that have passed, and in the hundreds of talks that Lane has given, scores of people have come up to her to tell her that forgiveness in their own lives had seemed unattainable. But after listening to her story, they know that they can now forgive those who have hurt them.

"I know it's a powerful script, but I don't take any credit for it because it is not the script I wanted," Lane says. "It's a script written by the Holy Spirit to help people understand the importance of forgiveness."

Act!

Go back to the first point in the Reflect! section. Ask God for mercy and help. Decide what action you need to take.

▶ In the Spotlight
Acknowledge, Apologize, Make Amends

"Love your enemies," Jesus teaches (Matthew 5:44). This is not only difficult but also sometimes complex, because we may have hurt the one who has hurt us. Then loving the person who has done us harm may include asking for his or her forgiveness. And this may apply to groups as well as to individuals.

As an Israeli, Dalia Landau has lived her whole life in the midst of this complexity. Born in the 1940s, she grew up in the new state of Israel. In Israeli society, alienation between Jews and Arabs runs deep, and there is resentment and fear on both sides. From a lifetime of efforts to draw Jews and Arabs together, Dalia has discovered three steps toward healing.

Acknowledgment. "Competition over who has suffered more and who wronged whom more has torpedoed so many attempts at dialogue between Arabs and Jews," Dalia observes. This has its source "in the deep, universal longing for acknowledgment"—the desire for the other to recognize what I, what we, have suffered. Thus, it is essential to listen to the other person's story of pain. This listening to the other's story of suffering has to be freely given, Dalia says; it cannot be dependent on an assurance that the other side will reciprocate. Acknowledgment "is an act of love."

Apology. This seems very simple. "Everyone knows what an apology is," she says. Why, then, is it sometimes so hard? "I find it is because apology entails letting go of being right, and that is a huge sacrifice for most of us, especially when it comes to being right about the past."

Amends. This means "taking action, doing something small or big." Sometimes the most we can offer is something symbolic, a gesture of goodwill. "Amends does not necessarily mean restoration of the past, because that past most likely cannot be restored—and the restoration that seems just to one side may feel totally unjust to the other." Nevertheless, Dalia says, making amends "is a healing gesture, an action that addresses the pain of the past and helps transform it in the present toward the future."

In the face of great obstacles, Dalia and others in Israel pursue reconciliation with these three "A" words. "We may feel helpless and ask how we, ordinary human beings, can hope to make a difference in a situation that seems to become more entangled all the time. As I see it, the work begins in the individual heart. We stretch our hearts, throughout a lifetime, a little more and yet a little more, to include in empathy that particularly irritating next-door neighbor whose behavior is absolutely unacceptable."

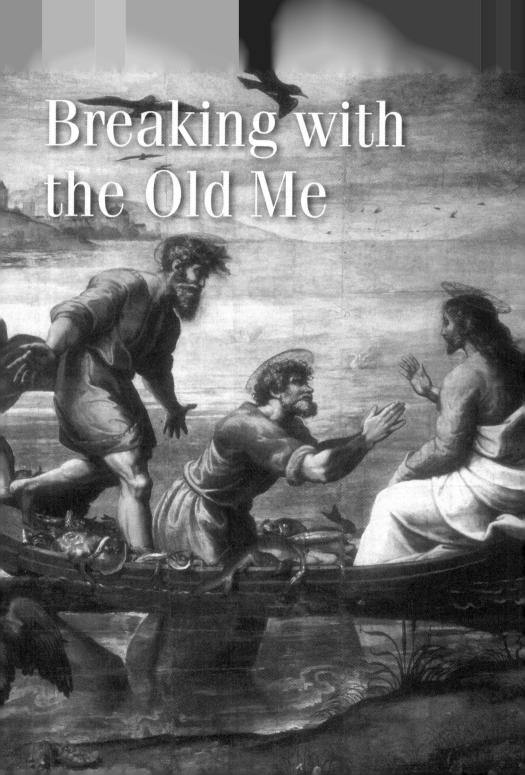

Breaking with
the Old Me

Romans 6:3-13; 5:1-2, 5-10

^{6:3}Do you not know that all of us who have been baptized into Christ Jesus were baptized into his death? ⁴Therefore we have been buried with him by baptism into death, so that, just as Christ was raised from the dead by the glory of the Father, so we too might walk in newness of life.

⁵For if we have been united with him in a death like his, we will certainly be united with

> The Holy Spirit is the love of the Father and the Son. To be given the Spirit is to become a sharer in their love.
> —St. Thomas Aquinas

him in a resurrection like his. ⁶We know that our old self was crucified with him so that the body of sin might be destroyed, and we might no longer be enslaved to sin. ⁷For whoever has died is freed from sin. ⁸But if we have died with Christ, we believe that we will also live with him. ⁹We know that Christ, being raised from the dead, will never die again; death no longer has dominion over him. ¹⁰The death he died, he died to sin, once for all; but the life he lives, he lives to God. ¹¹So you also must consider yourselves dead to sin and alive to God in Christ Jesus.

¹²Therefore, do not let sin exercise dominion in your mortal bodies, to make you obey their passions. ¹³No longer present your members to sin as instruments of wickedness, but present yourselves to God as those who have been brought from death to life, and present your members to God as instruments of righteousness. . . .

^{5:1}Since we are justified by faith, we have peace with God through our Lord Jesus Christ, ²through whom we have obtained access to this grace in which we stand; and we boast in our hope of sharing the glory of God. . . . ⁵and hope does not disappoint us, because God's love has been poured into our hearts through the Holy Spirit that has been given to us. ⁶For while we were still weak, at the right

time Christ died for the ungodly. [7] Indeed, rarely will anyone die for a righteous person—though perhaps for a good person someone might actually dare to die. [8] But God proves his love for us in that while we still were sinners Christ died for us. [9] Much more surely then, now that we have been justified by his blood, will we be saved through him from the wrath of God. [10] For if while we were enemies, we were reconciled to God through the death of his Son, much more surely, having been reconciled, will we be saved by his life.

News of a breakthrough medical procedure for a debilitating condition may be of only passing interest to the general population. But if you suffer from the condition, the report will grab *your* attention. Whether Paul's announcement of God's initiative to deal with human sinfulness strikes us as ho-hum or riveting depends, similarly, on our awareness of our need.

We might, then, ask ourselves a few questions before examining Paul's announcement. Do my cravings, resentments, impatience, or pride sometimes get out of hand? Have I become a truly integrated person, directing all my strengths and desires toward pleasing God and serving other people? Do I have the purity of heart and love for everyone that Jesus talks about in his Sermon on the Mount?

What would it take for me to become a person who quickly dismisses every temptation from my mind and stays on God's straight and narrow road, no matter what? Well, I would need power greater than my own, giving me the freedom to do what's right and good even when my needs, inclinations, and fears pull me away. Basically, that would require a down-to-the-roots-of-my-being transformation. You might almost say I would need to die and start afresh as a new person.

"Great!" says Paul. "If you know *that's* what you need, you're in a position to grasp the relevance of Jesus' death for you."

Although Jesus was certain that the Father willed him to offer his life to remove our sins, submitting to crucifixion was unimaginably hard. Yet Jesus resisted every temptation to turn off the road that led to the cross. Just look at his prayer in Gethsemane on the night of his arrest: "Father, for you all things are possible; remove this cup from me; yet, not what I want, but what you want" (Mark 14:36). Escape would have involved only a twenty-minute jog up and over the Mount of Olives into the Judean wilderness, but Jesus hunkered down and waited for his enemies to come and arrest him.

Because Jesus accepted death rather than following any temptation to deviate from God's will, Paul can say that "the death he died, he died to sin, once for all" (Romans 6:10). Now, for each of us needing to make a new start at living as the persons God created us to be, Jesus' death to sin has huge implications, *because he shares it with us*. When we come to faith in him and are baptized—immersed in him—we are plunged into his death. His unshakable commitment to doing his Father's will embraces us. His death becomes our death. With him, *we* die to sin. We experience a radical break with our old self, the "old me" attuned to sin and resistant to God.

Moreover, Jesus shares with us his resurrection from the dead. Having taken hold of us in baptism, he raises us up with himself into his own eternal life with God (Ephesians 2:6). And because we are united to Jesus in his resurrection, God fills us with the Holy Spirit—the power of his love—that he eternally pours out on his Son. "God's love has been poured into our hearts through the Holy Spirit" (Romans 5:5).

And then the Spirit begins to redirect our desires and longings toward God and toward the good things he wants us to be doing in this world (Ephesians 2:10). An eagerness to do God's will springs up in us. We experience a buoyancy that enables us to rise above contrary tendencies and orient ourselves toward loving God and other people as well as a resilience that enables us to move through difficulties toward the goals God sets for us (Philippians 2:13). In this way God is offering us a change of heart, a new life.

Our first step in response to God's offer is to believe what Jesus has done for us, to open our hearts to it, to determinedly take hold of it. "You . . . must consider yourselves dead to sin and alive to God in Christ Jesus" (Romans 6:11).

We also need to take action. "Do not let sin exercise dominion in your mortal bodies" (Romans 6:12). What God has done through Jesus does not replace our efforts; it makes them possible. There's nothing magical in our transformation, because it is *ours*. We become the persons we are meant to be by living the lives God gives us to live. In a mysterious way, God's grace and our efforts combine. God is creating us anew, empowering us, changing us, as we continue to live our lives, make our decisions, and deal with the difficulties we meet. The initiative is with God, but it is up to us to respond.

> The initiative is with God, but it is up to us to respond.

The transformation begins at baptism, and its outworking extends through our entire lives. The power of the Spirit in us is great, but the process of transformation is uneven. We do experience healing of our hearts and minds, but while some weaknesses to temptation disappear, others remain. Each of us is like a house getting a makeover that doesn't proceed according to a formula. A couple of rooms are quickly renovated, the attic is cleared out, the water in the basement is drained, but other parts of the building remain depressingly the same. The garage is still an embarrassment; the bathrooms need to be remodeled. Despite our efforts, we may go on being pretty much the same gossipy, greedy, gluttonous person we have always been. In some areas, the increments of change are so small that it would take a millennium to become the loving, generous, and humble person we would like to be. Discouragement becomes a temptation.

Here it is crucial to trust in God. He has his particular way of carrying out the renovations in each house. Whatever his way of working with us, he has demonstrated his total commitment to our transformation. "I went to the cross so that you could have a new life," Jesus reminds us. "Did you think I was going to abandon you at any point in the process?" Reread Romans 5:5-10!

Understand!

1. Paul tells us that Jesus "died for us" (Romans 5:8). In what ways do people die for each other, literally or figuratively? Has anyone ever died for you in any sense? What impact has this had on your life?

_____

_____

_____

_____

_____

2. We are "justified by faith," Paul says (Romans 3:28). He means that we are set right with God by taking hold of what God has done for us through Jesus ("We have been justified by his blood"—5:9) rather than through our own actions or merits. Paul is not denying that we need to respond to God's saving love (for example, see Philippians 2:12-13). He *is* denying that our relationship with God is founded on anything except God's free love for us. How does this make a difference in your experience of peace (Romans 5:1) and hope (5:1-10)?

_____

_____

_____

_____

_____

3. Paul tells us that through baptism into Christ, we have been freed from sin (Romans 6:7), and so we should regard ourselves as dead to it (6:11). Yet he also tells us, "Do not let sin exercise dominion in your mortal bodies, to make you obey their passions" (6:12), which assumes that we still experience sinful tendencies. Putting these pieces of evidence together, what picture can you draw of our condition with regard to sin once we are baptized into Christ?

_____

_____

_____

_____

_____

4. Paul declares that now we can "walk in newness of life" (Romans 6:4). What does this new life look like? See, for example, Galatians 5:22-23. Where do you experience this newness of life? How might you open yourself up to more of it?

_____

_____

_____

_____

_____

5. "God proves his love for us in that while we still were sinners Christ died for us" (Romans 5:8). Why do you think that God loves us so much?

_____

_____

_____

_____

_____

▶ In the Spotlight
An Angry God?

"Now that we have been justified by his blood, will we be saved through him from the wrath of God" (Romans 5:9). At first Paul might seem to be saying that Jesus, who is merciful, has saved us from God, who is wrathful. But a contrast between an angry Father and a compassionate Son is far from Paul's thinking.

Paul speaks of God, the Father of Jesus Christ, as "the Father of mercies" (2 Corinthians 1:3). And Jesus, far from being a contrast to the Father, is "the image of God" (2 Corinthians 4:4). Jesus makes the Father's love for us visible. It was in fulfillment of the Father's merciful plan for us that Jesus lowered himself to our human condition and laid down his life for us on the cross (Philippians 2:5-11).

But if the Father is compassionate, what does Paul mean by "the wrath of God"? How can God be infinitely merciful and frighteningly angry at the same time? The apparent contradiction begins to clear up when we see that speaking of God's "wrath" is a way of expressing his unalterable opposition to sin. God uncompromisingly rejects everything that warps and perverts his good creation, especially his human creation—everything that drains away the love, peace, and joy that he intends for humanity. The "wrath of God" is his commitment to completely destroy sin. It is with this sense of the wrath of God that Paul says, "The wrath of God is revealed from heaven against all ungodliness and wickedness of those who by their wickedness suppress the truth" (Romans 1:18). God's wrath is revealed in his bringing judgment on sin.

The New Testament writers teach that God is incomprehensibly loving toward sinners and uncompromisingly wrathful toward sin. If we cling to our sins, we cling to that which is under God's judgment, that which is the object of his wrath. It is our disastrous connection with sin that God has set out to change by sending his Son into the world. Jesus has come to deliver us from our sins. This moves us from a condition of experiencing God's wrath to one of experiencing his love (see Colossians 1:13-14). The depth of God's love for us is measured by the cost he has paid to deliver us: the life of his own Son. God wanted so badly to free us from being under the wrath that falls on sin "that he gave his only Son, so that everyone who believes in him may not perish but may have eternal life" (John 3:16).

Grow!

1. In Romans 6:6, 12, and 13, "sin" does not mean a wrong act but a power that pulls us into wrongdoing. Where in your life do you experience sin in this sense?

_____

_____

_____

_____

_____

2. "Hope does not disappoint us" (Romans 5:5). What are the situations in which you tend to get discouraged? How does Paul's message in Romans 5:5-10 speak to you in those situations? Consider especially Romans 5:8: "God proves his love for us in that while we still were sinners Christ died for us." What situation in your life would you handle differently if you were more deeply aware of this reality?

_____

_____

_____

_____

_____

3. Paul speaks about what God did for us and in us when we were baptized. The Sacrament of Reconciliation is a way of getting in touch anew with what happened when we were baptized. If you were to think of Confession as a renewal of baptism as Paul talks about in Romans 6:3-13, how might you change your approach to it?

_____

_____

_____

_____

_____

4. "God's love has been poured into our hearts through the Holy Spirit" (Romans 5:5). What has made you aware of the depth of God's love for you? What effect should that have on how you live today? How could you open yourself more fully to the love of the Holy Spirit?

_____

_____

_____

_____

_____

5. This reading is not primarily a call to repentance and a change of heart. Still, you can ask yourself, "What call to repentance and change of heart do I sense from God as I read Paul's words?"

_____

_____

_____

_____

_____

▶ In the Spotlight
The Experience of God's Grace

"Consider yourselves dead to sin and alive to God in Christ Jesus," St. Paul writes. "Therefore, do not let sin exercise dominion in your mortal bodies" (Romans 6:11, 12). This is a call to an experience of God's grace that, in some areas, may involve a long struggle.

Mark Houck first made contact with pornography when he was ten years old. It quickly became a part of his life.

Midway through his college years, Mark went to Confession. It was a profoundly liberating experience but only a beginning. "The Lord would prompt me to come back hundreds upon hundreds of times before I finally would be able to say that I was free from my pornography addiction and all its secondary effects of masturbation and disordered sexual thoughts and fantasies." Almost immediately, Mark resumed his use of pornography. "I felt empty inside and in need of much healing and forgiveness."

Some years later, Mark was brought up short by a pastor who warned him that his salvation was in jeopardy if he continued on the same path. Soon after, Mark signed a chastity pledge at a conference of young adults. "I wish I could tell you that this is all it took for the scales to fall from my eyes. But I needed to continue to make progress by making better choices."

Among these choices was resolving not to receive Communion in a state of serious sin and to get rid of all videos and magazines containing "pornographic triggers." "As I removed the unchaste materials," Mark says, "slowly I started to experience periods of freedom from lust. I began, also, to see the great benefit of frequent confession and Communion to safeguarding my purity. I felt peace knowing that I was in a state of grace and that I was able to hear and feel God's constant presence. I felt an interior joy, the kind of joy that comes from the assurance that God is in charge of my life and that wherever I go, he is with me."

Meeting the woman he hoped to marry spurred Mark to make the final sprint to the goal of freedom from sexual sin. "I had a deep desire to be set free from this sin prior to entering the sacrament of holy matrimony. The Eucharist was the only sure way I could become that sincere gift that I longed to be for my future bride. I know beyond any doubt that the graces I receive from daily Mass and frequent confession are the primary reason for my freedom from sexual sin. I believe in my heart that the virtue of chastity can be obtained, and maintained, solely through the grace of God."

Reflect!

1. Look back at Psalm 51 and notice how much the psalmist asks from God. How much of God's answer is found in our reading from Romans? In what ways is Paul's announcement God's response to your own prayer to God?

2. Reflect on these other statements by Paul about how the Spirit is at work in those who are baptized into Jesus Christ.

God has done what the law, weakened by the flesh, could not do: by sending his own Son in the likeness of sinful flesh, and to deal with sin, he condemned sin in the flesh, so that the just requirement of the law might be fulfilled in us, who walk not according to the flesh but according to the Spirit. For those who live according to the flesh set their minds on the things of the flesh, but those who live according to the Spirit set their minds on the things of the Spirit. To set the mind on the flesh is death, but to set the mind on the Spirit is life and peace. For this reason the mind that is set on the flesh is hostile to God; it does not submit to God's law—indeed it cannot, and those who are in the flesh cannot please God.

But you are not in the flesh; you are in the Spirit, since the Spirit of God dwells in you. Anyone who does not have the Spirit of Christ does not belong to him. But if Christ is in you, though the body is dead because of sin, the Spirit is life because of righteousness. If the Spirit of him who raised Jesus from the dead dwells in you, he who raised Christ from the dead will give life to your mortal bodies also through his Spirit that dwells in you.

So then, brothers and sisters, we are debtors, not to the flesh, to live according to the flesh—for if you live according to the flesh, you will die; but if by the Spirit you put to death the deeds of the body, you will live. (Romans 8:3-13)

Do you not know that your body is a temple of the Holy Spirit within you, which you have from God, and that you are not your own? For you were bought with a price; therefore glorify God in your body. (1 Corinthians 6:19-20)

Now the Lord is the Spirit, and where the Spirit of the Lord is, there is freedom. And all of us, with unveiled faces, seeing the glory of the Lord as though reflected in a mirror, are being transformed into the same image from one degree of glory to another; for this comes from the Lord, the Spirit. (2 Corinthians 3:17-18)

The fruit of the Spirit is love, joy, peace, patience, kindness, generosity, faithfulness, gentleness, and self-control. (Galatians 5:22-23)

▶ In the Spotlight
Peace through Our Lord Jesus Christ

Some years ago, when he was a deacon and director of the chaplaincy at Holy Cross Hospital in Detroit, Father Joseph Marquis was asked to see a man in the psychiatric unit. The patient, a large gentle man in his thirties, told Deacon Joseph about a dream in which Jesus appeared to him and told him he was going to die—and that he should go to Confession.

"Jeremy (not his real name) asked me if I thought he was crazy," Deacon Joseph said. "I told him that God sometimes speaks to us through dreams."

Deacon Joseph assured Jeremy that he would contact a priest to hear his confession right away. Since he said he had not been to Confession for many years, the deacon asked if he would like to prepare for it, and he agreed.

Jeremy told the deacon his life story. At the center of it was a gaping wound. "His father began to sexually abuse him when he was six years old and continued until he was in his teens. Then the father deserted the family. Jeremy had lived with shame his whole life. He had never developed a normal relationship with a woman. More than once he had tried to kill himself. In fact, he had been feeling suicidal yet again, and it was because of his pleas for help that he was admitted to the psychiatric ward this time. After listening to him at length, I told him that in my opinion, he had been sinned against in life far more than he had sinned."

The priest came in the afternoon, heard Jeremy's confession, and gave him absolution. The next day Deacon Joseph found Jeremy relieved but troubled. "Jesus had appeared to him in a dream again," Deacon Joseph recounted. "The Lord had a warm look on his face, Jeremy said, and he gave him a hug—and told him that he was going to die that night."

The deacon and Jeremy sat together for about an hour, and Jeremy expressed his forgiveness toward his father. As the deacon left the unit, he let the staff know about the dream that had made Jeremy think that he was about to die.

The following morning, Deacon Joseph returned to the psychiatric unit and found that the mental health staff was stunned. Jeremy had indeed died during the night. The staff had tried to revive him but without success. Later, an autopsy revealed that he had succumbed to an undiagnosed congenital heart anomaly.

"Since we are justified by faith," Paul writes, "we have peace with God through our Lord Jesus Christ." (Romans 5:1). While none of the paths to this peace are merely ordinary, some seem more extraordinary than others.

Act!

Sit quietly for some good period of time in a place that helps you become aware of God's presence. Ask him to show you the love that has been poured into your heart through the Holy Spirit that has been given to you.

▶In the Spotlight
The Wondrous Love of God

The American folk hymn "What Wondrous Love Is This" expresses amazement at Jesus' sacrifice of himself for us. Composed in the American South, it was first published in 1811 and later attributed to Alexander Means, a Methodist pastor. Here are three of the six verses.

What wondrous love is this, O my soul, O my soul!
What wondrous love is this, O my soul!
What wondrous love is this that caused the Lord of
    bliss!
To bear the dreadful curse for my soul, for my soul!
To bear the dreadful curse for my soul!

When I was sinking down, sinking down, sinking down;
When I was sinking down, sinking down,
When I was sinking down beneath God's righteous
    frown,
Christ laid aside his crown for my soul, for my soul!
Christ laid aside his crown for my soul!

Ye friends of Zion's king, join His praise, join His praise;
Ye friends of Zion's king, join His praise;
Ye friends of Zion's king, with hearts and voices sing,
And strike each tuneful string in His praise, in His
    praise!
And strike each tuneful string in His praise!

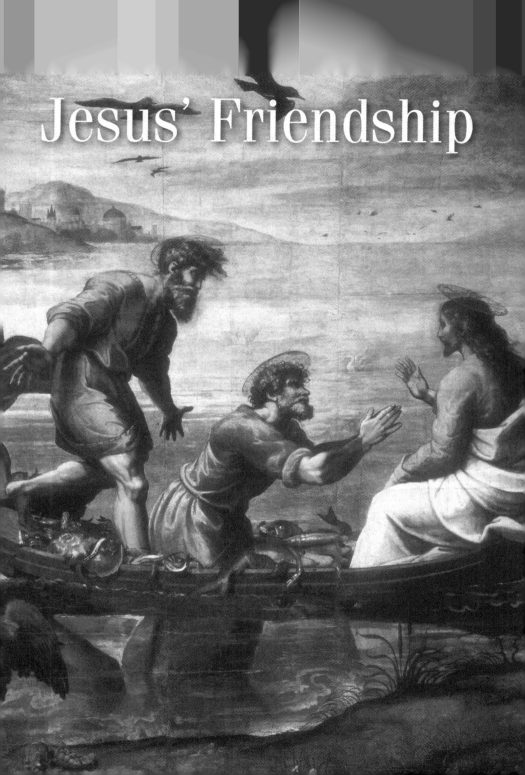

Jesus' Friendship

John 21:9-22

21:9When they had gone ashore, they saw a charcoal fire there, with fish on it, and bread. 10Jesus said to them, "Bring some of the fish that you have just caught." 11So Simon Peter went aboard and hauled the net ashore, full of large fish, a hundred fifty-three of them; and though there were so many, the net was not torn. 12Jesus said to them, "Come and have breakfast." Now none of the disciples dared to ask him, "Who are you?" because they knew it was the Lord.

> Jesus does not exclude anyone from his friendship.
> —Pope Benedict XVI

13Jesus came and took the bread and gave it to them, and did the same with the fish. 14This was now the third time that Jesus appeared to the disciples after he was raised from the dead.

15When they had finished breakfast, Jesus said to Simon Peter, "Simon son of John, do you love me more than these?" He said to him, "Yes, Lord; you know that I love you." Jesus said to him, "Feed my lambs." 16A second time he said to him, "Simon son of John, do you love me?" He said to him, "Yes, Lord; you know that I love you." Jesus said to him, "Tend my sheep." 17He said to him the third time, "Simon son of John, do you love me?" Peter felt hurt because he said to him the third time, "Do you love me?" And he said to him, "Lord, you know everything; you know that I love you." Jesus said to him, "Feed my sheep. 18Very truly, I tell you, when you were younger, you used to fasten your own belt and to go wherever you wished. But when you grow old, you will stretch out your hands, and someone else will fasten a belt around you and take you where you do not wish to go." 19(He said this to indicate the kind of death by which he would glorify God.) After this he said to him, "Follow me."

20Peter turned and saw the disciple whom Jesus loved following them; he was the one who had reclined next to Jesus at the supper and had said, "Lord, who is it that is going to betray you?" 21When Peter saw him, he said to Jesus, "Lord, what about him?" 22Jesus said to him, "If it is my will that he remain until I come, what is that to you? Follow me!"

Jesus of Nazareth and Simon, son of Jonah, also known as Peter, were friends. Peter was a fisherman, yet Jesus called him to a leadership role among his disciples. Peter was gifted with remarkable insight into Jesus (Matthew 16:15-19), but he had ideas about Jesus' ministry that ran contrary to Jesus' own, and the two men clashed (Mark 1:35-38; Matthew 16:21-23).

Early in his relationship with Jesus, Peter told him, "Go away from me, Lord, for I am a sinful man!" (Luke 5:8). Jesus' presence must have evoked a sense of guilt in Peter, but Jesus declined his plea and promised to make him a fisher of men (5:9-10).

That glimpse by Peter into the darkness in his own heart was only the initial stage of a journey to a realistic self-assessment. Yet despite his protestation, Peter still saw himself as a loyal disciple. On the evening before Jesus died, Peter assured Jesus that he would accompany him even to death (Mark 14:27-31). Peter's braggadocio was ill founded. An hour or so later, menaced by a hostile crowd, he would deny having any relationship with Jesus (John 13:36-38; 18:15-18, 25-27).

Three days later, when Jesus rose from the dead, one of the first items on his agenda was to confront Peter (Luke 24:34; 1 Corinthians 15:4-5). We have no transcript of the meeting, but it is easy to imagine how abject Peter was (consider Mark 14:72). Whatever Jesus said, it must have included an offer of forgiveness, for the two emerged from the encounter with their friendship restored. This brings us to the present scene.

After Jesus' resurrection, Peter and several other disciples go back to their homes along the Sea of Galilee. One night they go fishing on the lake. They don't catch anything, but in the morning as they are returning, they see Jesus standing on the shore. He tells them to lower their nets. When they do, they catch a huge number of fish. In a burst of enthusiasm, Peter dives into the water and swims to Jesus while the others bring the boat to land. Jesus cooks a breakfast of grilled fish. After the meal, he takes Peter aside for the conversation in our reading. It is the last time the two of them talk with each other one-on-one in the Gospels.

Jesus' question—"Do you love me?"—touches Peter in his still very sensitive spot, his painful memory of having denied Jesus. But Jesus is probing the wound only to heal. By asking the question three times, he gives Peter the opportunity to replace his threefold denial with a threefold affirmation.

> Only Peter's failure could enable him to see himself realistically.

Jesus' triple response, in turn, points Peter toward what he must do to demonstrate his restored love: care for Jesus' other followers. For Peter, the fulfillment of this leadership role will not be something that feeds his ego. After his denial of Jesus and Jesus' restoration of their friendship, Peter's exercise of his ministry will be an expression of gratitude to Jesus, a means of showing Jesus that he really *does* love him. Soon Jesus will no longer be physically present, but Peter will experience the continuation of their friendship as he goes about teaching and encouraging his fellow believers—perhaps the way a widow might experience her husband's presence as she carries on raising their children.

Peter's relationship with Jesus will be on firmer ground after his failure, built no longer on Peter's vain assessment of his own strength and courage but on his experience of Jesus' forgiveness and kindness. Only Peter's failure could enable him to see himself realistically— and convince him that Jesus knew him better than he knew himself.

Shameful as Peter's failing of Jesus was, it will now give his service to Jesus a distinctive quality. Peter will be conscious of the fact that his role of leadership is not only a gift from Jesus, but also a gift that has been restored after he forfeited it. Surely this will infuse Peter's ministry with a quality of mercy toward others that it might otherwise have lacked, as Peter "pays forward" the kindness he has received.

Jesus took the long view of Peter's life. From the beginning he looked into Peter and saw the bad and the good, the weakness and the pride that blinded him to it, and his potential for great love. He took Peter as he was, knowing what Peter could become. This touches on the most remarkable aspect of Jesus' friendship with Peter and the other men and women he called to follow him. He invited them to follow him knowing in advance that they would sometimes fail him. But he offered them his friendship so that they might become the men and women they wanted to be—men and women who loved and served him with their whole lives. Jesus made them his friends so that he might *truly* make them his friends, because his friendship with them was the only way they could become his true friends.

In the same way, Jesus calls us today. As we meet the challenges that arise in our following him, we discover things about ourselves that we do not like—weaknesses and sins. The dimension of our sins that comes to grieve us the most is our disloyalty and ingratitude toward him. For us, as for Peter, Jesus' friendship becomes the deepest motivation for repentance and change of heart. Jesus shows himself to be the friend beyond all friends who enables us to be true friends with him—the very thing that we desire as we come to know him more deeply.

Understand!

1. What might be the significance of Jesus' cooking breakfast for his disciples (John 21:9-13)?

_____

_____

_____

_____

_____

_____

2. Peter's conversation with Jesus takes place in the context of a meal. Jesus had shared many meals with his disciples, including a very unusual one that, like this one, took place along the shore of the Sea of Galilee (see John 6, especially verses 1 to 14). How might a recollection of that earlier meal help us see a deeper meaning in the present scene?

_____

_____

_____

_____

_____

3. "You are my friends," Jesus says to his disciples the night before he dies (John 15:14). From our reading, and other passages in the Gospels about Peter, what is the basis of the friendship between Jesus and Peter? Does Peter seem to grow in his friendship with Jesus over time? What is involved in growing in friendship with Jesus?

_____

_____

_____

_____

_____

_____

4. Jesus first asks Peter if he loves him "more than these," that is, more than the other disciples (John 21:15). Why doesn't Peter answer this part of Jesus' question? Can we gain some insight by comparing this situation to an earlier one from Mark 14:29?

_____

_____

_____

_____

_____

5. Why do you think that Peter asks Jesus about his plans for the other disciple (John 21:20-21)? Why doesn't Jesus tell him (verse 22)?

_____

_____

_____

_____

_____

▶ In the Spotlight
Not Yet Perfect

After Peter's restoration by Jesus and the coming of the Holy Spirit, Peter demonstrated courage in the face of physical intimidation and abuse (Acts 4). But it is worth remembering that he was not instantly and totally transformed. Some years later, under pressure in a difficult situation, he wavered and backed off from doing what was right. At least that was St. Paul's view of how Peter handled an important pastoral situation (see Galatians 2:11-14).

Yet Peter persevered in facing his weaknesses and trying to serve the sheep that Jesus had given him to shepherd. In the end, he gave his life in testimony to his friend. Ancient sources attest that Peter died as a Christian martyr by crucifixion in Rome around the year 66. Archaeology tends to confirm the long-standing tradition that the Basilica of St. Peter is built over his tomb.

Grow!

1. Is friendship with Jesus a too familiar way of thinking about your relationship with him? How would one distinguish an authentic from an inauthentic understanding of having Jesus as one's friend?

_____

_____

_____

_____

_____

2. Who have been your friends? Why do you regard them as friends? How do your friendships help you understand Jesus' friendship with you? What kinds of things have you had to work out in relationships with your friends? How are these issues similar to those that arise in your friendship with Jesus?

_____

_____

_____

_____

_____

_____

3. In your life, what is undermining your friendship with Jesus? What might you do about it?

_____

_____

_____

_____

_____

_____

4. Jesus asks you the question he put to Peter in John 21:15-17: "Do you love me?" How do you answer it?

_____

_____

_____

_____

_____

_____

5. Jesus enables Peter to complete his repentance for having denied Jesus by giving him the opportunity to reaffirm his love. Then Jesus gives him a task to carry out for him—to care for Jesus' other followers. Whom is he asking you to serve on his behalf?

_____

_____

_____

_____

_____

_____

▶ In the Spotlight
The Bridge Judas Chose Not to Cross

When Jesus was arrested, his disciples abandoned him to his fate. After his resurrection, it was only by his forgiveness that they could resume their vocation as his followers. This was especially true of Peter, who had explicitly denied knowing Jesus.

One disciple, however, did not receive forgiveness—the one who betrayed him. Some time between Jesus' arrest on Thursday night and his resurrection on Sunday morning, Judas committed suicide (Matthew 27:3-5). He recognized that he had done something seriously wrong. Did he then despair of forgiveness? Indeed, was his sin so heinous that forgiveness was impossible?

Jesus does speak of an unforgivable sin (Mark 3:29). In context, this sin was identifying Jesus' acts of mercy as workings of the devil. Such a rejection of God is unforgivable, not because God is unwilling to forgive, but because the one who thinks that an expression of God's mercy is the work of Satan has taken a position from which he or she will never seek forgiveness. But whatever Judas thought of Jesus at the end, he does not seem to have considered him to be a tool of the devil. Judas' last words about Jesus declare that he was "innocent" (Matthew 27:4). In fact, it was the realization that he had betrayed an innocent man that led him to take his own life.

Not only was Judas' sin forgivable, but it may even be that Jesus left him with something that might have helped him find his way back to him. When Judas led the arrest party to Gethsemane, Jesus said to him, "Judas, is it with a kiss that you are betraying the Son of Man?" (Luke 22:48). These words were not a damnation but a reproach. Indeed, it was a very personal reproach, which began, as many conversations between Jesus and Judas must have begun, with Jesus addressing him by name: "Judas." The reproach is in the form of a rhetorical question, underlining the terrible betrayal of friendship: "Are you actually betraying me with a sign of affection?" Yet although the question was rhetorical, it was also real. Jesus was calling Judas, even at the last moment, to reconsider what he was doing.

Afterward, when Judas realized the gravity of his sin, could Jesus' reproach—so personal, so sad—have led him to reflect on his master's love for him? Could that recollection—that word "Judas"—have been a bridge back to Jesus? It seems possible. But Judas chose not to cross that bridge.

Reflect!

1. Compare our reading in this session with the following account of Jesus and Peter earlier in their relationship. The incident takes place perhaps a couple of years before the scene in our present reading. What similarities do you find? How does Peter's relationship with Jesus develop from this earlier encounter?

Once while Jesus was standing beside the lake of Gennesaret, and the crowd was pressing in on him to hear the word of God, he saw two boats there at the shore of the lake; the fishermen had gone out of them and were washing their nets. He got into one of the boats, the one belonging to Simon, and asked him to put out a little way from the shore. Then he sat down and taught the crowds from the boat. When he had finished speaking, he said to Simon, "Put out into the deep water and let down your nets for a catch." Simon answered, "Master, we have worked all night long but have caught nothing. Yet if you say so, I will let down the nets." When they had done this, they caught so many fish that their nets were beginning to break. So they signaled their partners in the other boat to come and help them. And they came and filled both boats, so that they began to sink. But when Simon Peter saw it, he fell down at Jesus' knees, saying, "Go away from me, Lord, for I am a sinful man!" For he and all who were with him were amazed at the catch of fish that they had taken; and so also were James and John, sons of Zebedee, who were partners with Simon. Then Jesus said to Simon, "Do not be afraid; from now on you will be catching people." (Luke 5:1-10)

2. Consider Jesus' declaration below of his friendship to his disciples at the Last Supper. What is his understanding of friendship? How do you experience Jesus' friendship?

"As the Father has loved me, so I have loved you; abide in my love. If you keep my commandments, you will abide in my love, just as I have kept my Father's commandments and abide in his love. I have said these things to you so that my joy may be in you, and that your joy may be complete. This is my commandment, that you love one another as I have loved you. No one has greater love than this, to lay down one's life for one's friends. You are my friends if you do what I command you. I do not call you servants any longer, because the servant does not know what the master is doing; but I have called you friends, because I have made known to you everything that I have heard from my Father." (John 15:9-15)

3. It was Paul who wrote the following words, but they could have been spoken by Peter. Could they also be spoken by you?

It is no longer I who live, but it is Christ who lives in me. And the life I now live in the flesh I live by faith in the Son of God, who loved me and gave himself for me. (Galatians 2:20)

▶ In the Spotlight
An Encounter Triggered by Mercy

In 2001, Cardinal Jorge Mario Bergoglio—now Pope Francis— spoke at the presentation of a book by Father Luigi Giussani, the founder of the Communion and Liberation movement. The book, Cardinal Bergoglio said,

> is the description of that initial experience . . . of wonder which arises in . . . the exceptionally human and divine presence and gaze of Jesus Christ. . . . Everything in our life today, just as in Jesus' time, begins with an encounter. An encounter with this Man, the carpenter of Nazareth. . . .
>
> We cannot understand this dynamic of encounter which brings forth wonder and adherence if it has not been triggered . . . by mercy. Only someone who has encountered mercy, who has been caressed by the tenderness of mercy, is happy and comfortable with the Lord. . . . I dare to say that the privileged locus of the encounter is the caress of the mercy of Jesus Christ on my sin. . . .
>
> Christian morality is not a titanic effort of the will, the effort of someone who decides to be consistent and succeeds, a solitary challenge in the face of the world. No. Christian morality is simply a response. It is the heart-felt response to a surprising, unforeseeable, "unjust"

mercy. . . . The surprising, unforeseeable, "unjust" mercy
. . . of one who knows me, knows my betrayals and loves
me just the same, appreciates me, embraces me, calls me
again, hopes in me, and expects from me. This is why the
Christian conception of morality is a revolution; it is not
a never falling down but an always getting up again.

Act!

Go back to the Grow! section and reread question 3. What
is undermining your friendship with Jesus? What *will* you do
about it?

▶ In the Spotlight
Communion, Forgiveness, and Healing

The main item on Jesus' breakfast menu was grilled fish. But
notice also the bread. When the disciples came ashore, they saw
a charcoal fire, "with fish on it, and bread" (John 21:9). Then
"Jesus came and took the bread and gave it to them" (21:13).

The bread should catch our attention. It was along the shore
of the same lake that Jesus had multiplied bread (John 6:1-14).
This miraculous creation of bread was a foreshadowing of the
Eucharist, in which Jesus would give himself to his disciples.
With this background, the bread at this meal is a reminder of
the Eucharist. And thus the meal suggests a connection between
the Eucharist and Jesus and Peter's conversation. Their conversation of deep friendship is related to Jesus' gift of himself in
the Eucharist.

Thus, the scene of Jesus and Peter talking with each other as
friends stands as an image of the reconciliation with himself that

Jesus grants in the Eucharist. Certainly the Sacrament of Confession is the place in which we meet Jesus for the forgiveness of our sins—a necessary place of encounter if we have committed grave sins. But it is Jesus' presence in the Eucharist that is ultimately the source of all forgiveness and healing of heart and mind (*Catechism of the Catholic Church*, 1393).

The liturgies of the West and East reflect the awareness that by receiving Communion, we renew our relationship with the One who comes to forgive and transform us. Before Communion in the Roman liturgy, participants pray, "Lord, I am not worthy that you should enter under my roof, but only say the word and my soul shall be healed." In the Byzantine liturgy, participants pray a longer prayer before Communion, expressing faith that Jesus will forgive our sins and heal our inner being: "May the partaking of your holy mysteries, O Lord, be not for my judgment or condemnation but for the healing of soul and body. . . . I pray, make me worthy to receive for the remission of all my sins and for life everlasting. . . . O God, be merciful to me a sinner. O God, cleanse me of my sins and have mercy on me. O Lord, forgive me for I have sinned without number."

In the ceremony of reception, the Byzantine liturgy continues to point to Jesus in the Eucharist as the source of forgiveness. As the priest or deacon gives Communion to each recipient, he declares: "The servant / handmaid of God, partakes of the precious, most holy, and most pure body and blood of our Lord, God, and Savior Jesus Christ for the remission of his / her sins and for life everlasting. Amen."

Practical Pointers for Bible Discussion Groups

A Bible discussion group is another key that can help us unlock God's word. Participating in a discussion or study group—whether through a parish, a prayer group, or a neighborhood—offers us the opportunity to grow not only in our love for God's word but also in our love for one another. We don't have to be trained Scripture scholars to benefit from discussing and studying the Bible together. Bible study groups provide an environment in which we can worship and pray together and strengthen our relationships with other Christians. The following guidelines can help a group get started and run smoothly.

Getting Started

- Decide on a regular time and place to meet. Meeting on a regular basis allows the group to maintain continuity without losing momentum from the previous discussion.

- Set a time limit for each session. An hour and a half is a reasonable length of time in which to have a rewarding discussion on the material contained in each of the sessions in this guide. However, the group may find that a longer time is even more advantageous. If it is necessary to limit the meeting to an hour, select sections of the material that are of greatest interest to the group.

- Designate a moderator or facilitator to lead the discussions and keep the meetings on schedule. This person's role is to help preserve good group dynamics by keeping the discussion on track. He or she should help ensure that no one monopolizes the session and that each person—including the shyest or quietest individual—is offered an opportunity to speak. The group may want to ask members to take turns moderating the sessions.

- Provide enough copies of the study guide for each member of the group, and ask everyone to bring a Bible to the meetings. Each session's Scripture text and related passages for reflection are printed in full in the guides, but you will find that a Bible is helpful for looking up other passages and cross-references. The translation provided in this guide is the New Revised Standard Version (Catholic edition). You may also want to refer to other translations—for example, the New American Bible or the New Jerusalem Bible—to gain additional insights into the text.

- Try to stay faithful to your commitment and attend as many sessions as possible. Not only does regular participation provide coherence and consistency to the group discussions, but it also demonstrates that members value one another and are committed to sharing their lives with one another.

Session Dynamics

- Read the material for each session in advance, and take time to consider the questions and your answers to them. The single most important key to any successful Bible study is having everyone prepared to participate.

- As a courtesy to all members of your group, try to begin and end each session on schedule. Being prompt respects the other commitments of the members and allows enough time for discussion. If the group still has more to discuss at the end of the allotted time, consider continuing the discussion at the next meeting.

- Open the sessions with prayer. A different person could have the responsibility of leading the opening prayer at each session. The prayer can be a spontaneous one, a traditional prayer such as the Our Father, or one that relates to the topic of that particular meeting. The members of the group might also want to begin some of the meetings with a song or hymn. Whatever you choose, ask the Holy Spirit to guide your discussion and study of the Scripture text presented in that session.

- Contribute actively to the discussion. Let the members of the group get to know you, but try to stick to the topic so that you won't divert the discussion from its purpose. And resist the temptation to monopolize the conversation, so that everyone will have an opportunity to learn from one another.

- Listen attentively to everyone in the group. Show respect for the other members and their contributions. Encourage, support, and affirm them as they share. Remember that many questions have more than one answer and that the experience of everyone in the group can be enriched by considering a variety of viewpoints.

- If you disagree with someone's observation or answer to a question, do so gently and respectfully, in a way that shows that you value the person who made the comment, and then explain your own point of view. For example, rather than say, "You're wrong!" or "That's ridiculous!" try something like, "I think I see what you're getting at, but I think that Jesus was saying something different in this passage." Be careful to avoid sounding aggressive or argumentative. Then, watch to see how the subsequent discussion unfolds. Who knows? You may come away with a new and deeper perspective.

- Don't be afraid of pauses and reflective moments of silence during the session. People may need some time to think about a question before putting their thoughts into words.

- Maintain and respect confidentiality within the group. Safeguard the privacy and dignity of each member by not repeating what has been shared during the discussion session unless you have been given permission to do so. That way everyone will get the greatest benefit out of the group by feeling comfortable enough to share on a deep and personal level.

- End the session with prayer. Thank God for what you have learned through the discussion, and ask him to help you integrate it into your life.

The Lord blesses all our efforts to come closer to him. As you spend time preparing for and meeting with your small group, be confident in the knowledge that Christ will fill you with wisdom, insight, and grace and the ability to see him at work in your daily life.

Sources and Acknowledgments

Introduction

Pope Benedict XVI, Homily for the Synod of Bishops, October 5, 2008.

Session 1: Estranged Brothers Meet

Charles Dickens, *A Tale of Two Cities*.

W. Lee Humphreys, *Joseph and His Family* (Columbia, SC: University of South Carolina Press, 1988), 47.

Leo Tolstoy, *The Death of Ivan Ilych*, translated by Louise and Aylmer Maude. The story is available at http://www.ccel.org/ccel/tolstoy/ivan.html.

"The Struggle to Forgive" adapted from an anonymous article, "Forgiving the Unforgivable," in *The Word Among Us* magazine, April 2005. For information about the Divine Mercy devotion, contact the National Shrine of the Divine Mercy, Eden Hill, Stockbridge, MA. (800) 462-7426, www.marian.org.

Quotations from the Historical Institute of the Mercedarian Order, The Order of the Blessed Virgin Mary of Mercy (1218–1992): A Historical Synthesis. Mercedarian Library VI. (Rome 1997), 18-29; viewed in May 2014 on the Mercedarians' website: orderofmercy.org.

Session 2: A Man Had Two Sons

St. Augustine, *Confessions,* translated by Edward B. Pusey.

Arland J. Hultgren, *The Parables of Jesus: A Commentary* (Grand Rapids, MI: Eerdmans, 2000), 73, 76.

Adapted from Gretchen Traylor, "The Breath of Life," in *The Word Among Us*, Lent 2010.

Quotation regarding Charles de Foucauld from Robert Ellsberg, *All Saints* (New York: Crossroad, 1997), 524. Quoted words of Charles de Foucauld from Ellsberg and from Boniface Hanley, OFM, "Charles de Foucauld," in *No Strangers to Violence, No Strangers to Love* (Notre Dame, IN: Ave Maria, 1983), 73.

Byzantine prayer adapted from Mother Mary and Archimandrite Kallistos Ware, *The Lenten Triodion* (London: Faber and Faber, 1978), 120–21.

Session 3: A Sinner Prays for Forgiveness

St. Robert Bellarmine, *Explanatio in Psalmos*, Volume 1 (Parisiis: Ludocicus Vivès, 1877), translated by Kevin Perrotta, 340.

Dave Pivonka, TOR, *Hiking the Camino: 500 Miles with Jesus* (Cincinnati: Servant Books, 2009), 70–71. Used with permission of Franciscan Media.

Artur Weiser, *The Psalms* (Philadelphia: Westminster Press, 1962), 409.

Session 4: A True Cardiologist

Pope Francis, interview with Antonio Spadaro, SJ, September 2013, appearing in *America* magazine online, September 19, 2013.

St. Augustine, *The Lord's Sermon on the Mount*, translated by John J. Jepson, SS (Westminster, MD: Newman Press, 1948), 42–45.

Mary Healy, *Men and Women Are from Eden: A Study Guide to John Paul II's Theology of the Body* (Cincinnati: Servant Books, 2005), 45–47. Used with permission of Franciscan Media.

Account of Marietta Jaeger Lane adapted from Patrick O'Neill, "Marietta Jaeger Lane's Story: Mother Shares Loss of Daughter to Teach Forgiveness," accessed April 2014 at thejourneyofhope. blogspot.com/2011/03/mother-shares-loss-of-daughter-to-teach. html.

Dalia Landau, Jerusalem, Israel, unpublished paper, 2012.

Session 5: Breaking with the Old Me

St. Thomas Aquinas, *In Omnes S. Pauli Apostoli Epistulas Commentaria*, vol. 1. *Editio Septima Taurinensis* (Turin: Libraria Mariette, 1929), 68, translated by Kevin Perrotta.

Adapted from interviews with Mark Houck, "Many Victories," in Matt Fradd, ed., *Delivered: True Stories of Men and Women Who Turned from Porn to Purity* (San Diego: Catholic Answers Press, 2013). Used with permission of Catholic Answers.

Fr. Joseph Marquis, Sacred Heart Byzantine Catholic Church, Livonia, Michigan, unpublished interview with Kevin Perrotta, May 2014.

What Wondrous Love Is This, accessed at hymntime.com/tch/htm/w/h/a/whatwond.htm. An a capella rendition can be found on YouTube: "Blue Highway in Bristol" (youtube.com/watch?v=Nu9KjxaVEC4).

Session 6: Jesus' Friendship

Pope Benedict XVI, General Audience, August 30, 2006.

Cardinal Jorge Mario Bergoglio, April 27, 2001, speaking at presentation of book by Luigi Giussani, reported by Robert Moynihan, themoynihanletters.com/from-the-desk-of/letter-90 -editorial-on-popes-interview, accessed October 2013.

The Byzantine Catholic Metropolitan Church *Sui Juris* of Pittsburgh, *The Divine Liturgies of Our Holy Fathers John Chrysostom and Basil the Great,* 2006, 77–78, and *The Divine Liturgy of Our Holy Father John Chrysostom,* 2006, 92.

Visuals

Often our prayer can be enhanced by meditating on artwork that depicts a biblical scene. Here are visuals of some of the scenes included in this study that may help you as you pray with the text.

Session 1: Estranged Brothers Meet

James Tissot, *Joseph Converses with Judah, His Brother*:
http://www.wikipaintings.org/en/james-tissot/joseph-converses
-with-judah-his-brother#supersized-artistPaintings-242647

Horace Vernet: *Joseph's Coat*:
http://www.bbc.co.uk/arts/yourpaintings/paintings/
josephs-coat-209365

Session 2: A Man Had Two Sons

Rembrandt, *The Return of the Prodigal Son*:
http://www.hermitagemuseum.org/html_En/03/hm3_3_1_4d
.html.

Thomas Hart Benton, *Prodigal Son*:
http://amica.davidrumsey.com/luna/servlet/detail/
AMICO~1~1~40952~86275:Prodigal
-Son?sort=INITIALSORT_CRN%2COCS%2CAMICOID
&qvq=q:AMICOID%3DDMA_.1945.1%2B;sort:INITIALS
ORT_CRN%2COCS%2CAMICOID;lc:AMICO~1~1&mi=0&
trs=1

Ancient agricultural terraces in Israel/Palestine:
http://holylandphotos.org/browse
.asp?s=488,489,492&img=DLPLGP23

http://holylandphotos.org/browse
.asp?s=1,2,6,15,169&img=ICHJVS03

Session 6: Jesus' Friendship

Caravaggio, *The Denial of St. Peter*:
http://upload.wikimedia.org/wikipedia/commons/7/79/The
_Denial_of_Saint_Peter-Caravaggio_%281610%29.jpg

Caravaggio, *The Crucifixion of St. Peter*:
http://www.executedtoday.com/images/Crucifixion_of_Saint_
Peter_Caravaggio.jpg

the WORD among us ®
The *Spirit* of Catholic Living

This book was published by The Word Among Us. Since 1981, The Word Among Us has been answering the call of the Second Vatican Council to help Catholic laypeople encounter Christ in the Scriptures.

The name of our company comes from the prologue to the Gospel of John and reflects the vision and purpose of all of our publications: to be an instrument of the Spirit, whose desire is to manifest Jesus' presence in and to the children of God. In this way, we hope to contribute to the Church's ongoing mission of proclaiming the gospel to the world so that all people would know the love and mercy of our Lord and grow ever more deeply in love with him.

Our monthly devotional magazine, *The Word Among Us*, features meditations on the daily and Sunday Mass readings, and currently reaches more than one million Catholics in North America and another half million Catholics in one hundred countries around the world. Our book division, The Word Among Us Press, publishes numerous books, Bible studies, and pamphlets that help Catholics grow in their faith.

To learn more about who we are and what we publish, log on to our website at www.wau.org. There you will find a variety of Catholic resources that will help you grow in your faith.

Embrace His Word, Listen to God . . .

www.wau.org